Date Due

THE
REFERENCE
SHELF

SAVING
SOCIAL SECURITY

edited by JASON BERGER

THE REFERENCE SHELF

Volume 54, Number 4

THE H. W. WILSON COMPANY

New York   1982

THE REFERENCE SHELF

The books in this series contain reprints of articles, excerpts from books, and addresses on current issues and social trends in the United States and other countries. There are six separately bound numbers in each volume, all of which are generally published in the same calendar year. One number is a collection of recent speeches; each of the others is devoted to a single subject and gives background information and discussion from various points of view, concluding with a comprehensive bibliography. Books in the series may be purchased individually or on subscription.

Library of Congress Cataloging in Publication Data

Main entry under title:

Saving social security.

  (Reference shelf; v. 54, no. 4)
  Bibliography: p.
  1. Social security—United States—Addresses, essays, lectures.   I. Berger, Jason.   II. Series.
  HD7125.S28   1982   368.4′3′00973   82-13457
  ISBN 0-8242-0668-1

International Standard Book Number 0-8242-0668-1
PRINTED IN THE UNITED STATES OF AMERICA

CONTENTS

III. THE REFORM DEBATE

IV. PLENTY OF REACTION, BUT NO SOLUTION

THE SOCIAL SECURITY SYSTEM *

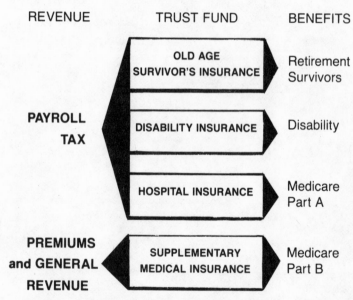

This figure shows the components of the Social Security system and how they are financed.

* Source: Appendix A, *Keeping Social Security Strong—Analysis and Recommendations.* By permission of the New York Office for the Aging.

PREFACE

On June 5, 1982, 350 senior citizens met in New York City to discuss the latest developments in the Social Security crisis. Sixty-three-year-old Esther Bernson spoke: "We're very, very, upset. We don't know what's in store. We're just living from day to day. It's very, very difficult." Representative Claude Pepper, the 81-year-old chairman of the House of Representatives Select Committee on Aging addressed the group. He promised: "We're not going to allow cuts in Social Security, and we are not going to allow cuts in Medicare. What we are fighting for today is to preserve those great institutions we've been building for a half a century to try to make life better for the elderly people of this country."[*]

He reminded the group that for nearly fifty years Americans have been paying their Social Security payroll tax expecting that, in return, the government would provide them, upon retirement, with a modest pension. The commitment, described by economists as an "entitlement," and recently by President Reagan as a "safety net" protecting the elderly from falling below the poverty level, is viewed by most Americans as a basic economic right, now being threatened.

In January 1982, American workers were astounded by the size of new Social Security deductions in paychecks—some exceed federal income tax deductions. Many were dismayed to learn that payroll deductions might even have to rise higher, that their retirement would be delayed, and that they could not hope to collect even what they paid into the system in their golden years.

Simply put, the Social Security fund is dangerously low. Never before have so many Americans been so concerned about Social Security. The reasons put forth are many: demographics (our population is growing older), inflation/recession, fraud, waste, double dipping, non-taxable Social Se-

[*] *New York Times.* Je. 5, '82. p 25+.

curity income, and the inadequacies in income transference. As these problems become even more evident and critical, past administrations and Congresses have refused to solve them in consideration of political repercussions.

President Reagan tried. He and his conservative advisers proposed what they called structural reforms in the system in the spring of 1981. Congress defeated his plan and the American public was no more enthusiastic about it. However, a minority in the country did praise the President for at least showing the courage to face the problems. A year later, a conservative coalition in Congress proposed another plan with substantial cuts in Social Security. That, too, was rejected by Congress. Thus, Americans are now receiving their Social Security checks temporarily funded under a system which can be compared to "borrowing from Peter to save Paul."

Section I of this compilation defines Social Security. Excerpts, written by a liberal historian, a news commentator, and an insurance executive discuss the growth of the system. Section II focuses on a wide range of problems inherent in the system. Section III examines the many and varied solutions offered, including the President's own plan. This is followed in Section IV with an analysis of the public response to President Reagan's proposals.

JASON BERGER

June 1982

I. SOCIAL SECURITY: WHAT IS IT?

EDITOR'S INTRODUCTION

*Is it an individual's responsibility to save for his own
retirement?*
Is it government's responsibility?
or
Is it a right all Americans are entitled to?

These were some of the questions raised in 1935 when the federal government assumed Social Security responsibility. These questions are now being raised once again as Americans are being forced to deal with the enormous cost of the burgeoning Social Security system.

Responding to fear that the retirement savings of elderly Americans could be wiped out by the Great Depression, Congress passed and President Franklin D. Roosevelt signed the historic Social Security Act of 1935. Thus the federal government became in effect an insurance agent legally requiring Americans and their employers to set aside funds for retirement. In the first article, a selection from his book, *The Coming of the New Deal,* Professor Arthur M. Schlesinger Jr. discusses the origins of the Social Security Act. For Schlesinger and others who advocated the legislation, the commitment of government to guarantee a minimum income for retirees, regardless of means, is a basic right to which all citizens are entitled.

In the second article, George J. Church, writing in *Time* Magazine, describes the Social Security system as it has evolved over the years. He shows how President Roosevelt's brainchild is not as he planned it, for it grew into a politically vulnerable giant on the verge of financial collapse.

In the third article, sociologist Eli Ginzberg, writing in *Scientific American,* appraises some alternatives for funding Social Security and he also calls for improvements in benefits for retirees. In outlining the basic mechanics of Social Security, he describes the different programs that were added to the system over 45 years.

The last article in this section examines the economic premises of income transference and its adverse effect on savings and the economy. Ashley Bladen, an insurance executive, writing in *Forbes*, maintains that such income should not be transferred, but put into productive investment to generate more income, thereby benefiting the economy of the country as a whole.

THE BIRTH OF SOCIAL SECURITY[1]

"We advocate," the Democratic platform of 1932 had remarked, "unemployment and old-age insurance under State laws." This declaration, with all its limitations, recognized the rising interest in both forms of public insurance—an interest visible for more than a generation in Europe and detectable for at least a decade in America. It recognized probably too the rising influence of Franklin Roosevelt, the single national political leader to identify himself with the social insurance cause. . . .

When the Committee on Economic Security came to the question of the aged, it adopted a national system of contributory old-age and survivors insurance without anxiety or fuss. In so doing, it took a venturesome step which contrasted strikingly with the caution shown in the case of unemployment compensation—and in spite of the fact that much more thought had been given to a national system for the unemployed than for the aged. One reason why the Committee could be more audacious here was the absence of state old-age insurance projects; there was no Wisconsin plan to create vested intellectual interests. Another was the fierce outside agitation for old-age pensions; though the Committee on Eco-

---

[1] Excerpt from the book, *The Coming of the New Deal*, by Arthur M. Schlesinger Jr. Sentry Edition, Houghton Mifflin Company. '58. p 303–15. Copyright Houghton Mifflin 1958. Reprinted by permission.

nomic Security had started work before Dr. Townsend's plan for $200 a month for everyone over sixty had developed momentum, yet the mounting Townsendite [lobbying group] clamor in late 1934 and early 1935 certainly improved the opportunity for inserting sweeping old-age insurance recommendations in the Social Security bill. Another—and perhaps decisive—reason was the conviction of the actuaries that old-age insurance on a state basis would be infeasible because of the great mobility of workers in the course of a lifetime.

In addition to the old-age insurance system, the Committee called for a program of assistance to the states for the needy aged. This recommendation was based on the provisions of the Dill-Connery bill of 1934. Parallel recommendations were made for federal aid to the states for the blind and for dependent children: and federal grants were proposed for maternal and child-health aid, and for the child-welfare and public-health services. On health insurance, the Committee made no recommendations for immediate legislation. For a moment in 1934 there had been a flurry of optimism on this point: Harry Hopkins had declared himself convinced that "with one bold stroke we could carry the American people with us, not only for unemployment insurance but for sickness and health insurance." But the usual pressure from the American Medical Association succeeded in killing staff proposals in the medical field. . . .

On January 15, 1935, the Committee on Economic Security transmitted its report to the President. Roosevelt already had his own views on Social Security. "There is no reason why everybody in the United States should not be covered," he once said to Miss Perkins. "I see no reason why every child, from the day he is born, shouldn't be a member of the social security system. . . . I don't see why not," he continued as Miss Perkins, appalled by the administrative problems of universal coverage, shook her head. "I don't see why not. Cradle to the grave—from the cradle to the grave they ought to be in a social insurance system."

He had in addition specific views about the character of a social insurance program. Thus he believed that public insurance should be built upon the same principles as private insurance. "If I have anything to say about it," he once remarked, "it will always be contributed, and I prefer it to be contributed, both on the part of the employer and the employee, on a sound actuarial basis. It means no money out of the Treasury." This meant a self-supporting system, financed by contributions and special taxes rather than out of the general tax revenue. Frances Perkins, arguing against employee contributions, pointed out that the employer shifted the payroll tax to the consumer in any case, so that employees were already paying their share; Tugwell, arguing against the payroll tax, pointed out that this amounted to a form of sales tax and meant that the system would be financed by those who could least afford it; but none of this argument availed. "I guess you're right on the economics," Roosevelt explained to another complainant some years later, "but those taxes were never a problem of economics. They are politics all the way through. We put those payroll contributions there so as to give the contributors a legal, moral, and political right to collect their pensions and their unemployment benefits. With those taxes in there, no damn politician can ever scrap my Social Security program."

On January 17, 1935, Roosevelt sent a message to Congress requesting Social Security legislation. On the same day Wagner introduced the draft bill in the Senate and Lewis, jointly with Congressman Robert L. Doughton of North Carolina, introduced it in the House. A few days later hearings began in both Senate and House. Early in February, the administration made an important change of front when Secretary Morgenthau, testifying before the House Ways and Means Committee, advocated a new financing plan for the old-age insurance system.

The Committee on Economic Security, confronting the problem of the aged, proposed a compulsory system of contributory payments by which workers could build up gradually their rights to annuities in their old age. This left the problem of persons on the verge of retirement who had had no past opportunity to contribute to their own old-age pensions. The best way in which these aging workers could be taken care of, the Committee concluded, was through the federal government's paying a share of the cost. By 1980, according to its estimate, the government would have to contribute to the old-age system around $1.4 billion a year. The Committee conceded that the creation of this commitment would impose a burden on future generations. But the alternative would be to increase reserves at a far higher rate and thus impose a double burden on the present generation, which would have to contribute not only to its own annuities but to the unearned annuities of people middle-aged or over. "The plan we advocate," said the Committee, "amounts to having each generation pay for the support of the people then living who are old."

Morgenthau had accepted the Committee plan and signed the report. Yet as he meditated the financing scheme, he began to feel a certain immorality, as he told the Ways and Means Committee, in the notion of "borrowing from the future to pay the costs." Roosevelt shared Morgenthau's disapproval. "It is almost dishonest," he told Frances Perkins, "to build up an accumulated deficit for the Congress of the United States to meet in 1980. We can't do that. We can't sell the United States short in 1980 any more than in 1935."

The Treasury alternative was to raise the rates of contribution and thereby build a much larger reserve fund, so that future needs could be met from the fund rather than by levies on current general revenue. This fund, Morgenthau suggested, could be applied to the reduction of the national debt. Roosevelt even supposed that it might eventually serve as the sole customer for federal bonds, thus freeing the government from reliance on private bankers. Under the original plan, the maximum size of the reserve fund would have been less than $12 billion; under the Treasury plan, it would amount to $50 billion by 1980. The Treasury plan had obvious disadvantages. It shifted the burden of providing for currently aging workers from the population as a whole to the younger wage-earners. "Our programs," said Abraham Epstein, "actually relieve the wealthy from their traditional obligation under the ancient poor laws." Moreover, the creation of so large a fund involved economic risks. As Alvin Hansen on the Technical Board and Marion Folsom of the Eastman Kodak Company on the Advisory Council pointed out, it would divert a large amount of money from consumer purchasing power; "that is bound," Folsom said, "to have a depressing effect on general conditions." And the problem of finding ways to invest $50 billion seemed packed with difficulties.

The self-sustaining theory of social insurance meant in effect that the poor had to pay most of the cost of keeping the poor. Yet, whether because of this or in spite of this, the House Committee quickly adopted the reserve system; probably the idea that private insurance should serve as the model was too compelling. Moreover, there was the political advantage which so impressed Roosevelt. Under the original plan, the old-age insurance system would be at the mercy of each succeeding Congress; while, with a vast reserve fund built up out of contributions, the people were in a sense creating a clear and present equity in their own retirement benefits. The existence of the reserve thus undoubtedly strenghtened the system politically. Yet the impact of the reserve on the business cycle—the withdrawal of large sums of money from the spending stream and the reliance on regressive taxation—doubtless added deflationary tendencies which later in the decade weakened the whole nation economically. In time, it appeared that the administration and the Congress had made the wrong decision in 1935.

While the friends of social security were arguing out the details of the program, other Americans were regarding the whole idea with consternation, if not with horror. Organized business had long warned against such pernicious notions. "Unemployment insurance cannot be placed on a sound financial basis," said the National Industrial Conference Board; it will facilitate "ultimate socialistic control of life and industry," said the National Association of Manufacturers. "Industry," observed Alfred Sloan of General Motors, "has every reason to be alarmed at the social, economic and financial implications. . . . The dangers are manifest." It will undermine our national life "by destroying initiative, discouraging thrift, and stifling individual responsibility" (James L. Donnelly of the Illinois Manufacturers' Association); it begins a pattern which "sooner or later will bring about the inevitable abandonment of private capitalism" (Charles Denby Jr., of the American Bar Association); "the downfall of Rome started with corn laws, and legislation of that type" (George P. Chandler of the Ohio Chamber of Commerce). With unemployment insurance no one would work; with old-age and survivors insurance no one would save; the result would be moral decay, financial bankruptcy and the collapse of the republic. One after another, business leaders appeared before House and Senate Committees to invest such dismal prophecies with what remained of their authority. . . .

A DEBT-THREATENED DREAM[2]

Ronald Reagan . . . called it "a political football" kicked around by "demagoguery" and "falsehoods." To one of the President's advisers it is "the most sacred cow we have around here." Democratic Senator James Sasser of Tennessee believes that "it might well be the dominant issue in this fall's campaigns." Even . . . Senate Republicans were pitted against House Republicans, to the glee of their Democratic adversaries, and a meeting of a blue-ribbon presidential commission degenerated into a partisan shouting match.

The subject is Social Security, the nation's biggest, broadest and probably most successful social program. To some 36 million people, nearly one American in every six, the Social Security system now provides a monthly check promising that old age, widowhood or disabling injury will not throw them into poverty. To 116 million others who pay Social Security taxes, the system offers assurance that they too will be taken care of when they become too old to work.

[2] Magazine article by George J. Church, contributor. *Time.* 118:16–27. My. 24, '82. Copyright 1982 by Time Inc. All rights reserved. Reprinted by permission.

But after more than 40 years during which such protection has been taken almost for granted, the nation faces a distressing question: Just how much Social Security can it afford? The answer: not as much as the formulas now written into law would provide in the future.

After decades of overambitious expansion, Social Security is quite simply running out of ready cash to get through the 1980s. Right now it is paying out in benefits $17,000 more than it collects in payroll taxes every minute of every hour of every day. At that rate, the trust fund on which 31.6 million pension checks are drawn every month will be nearly empty by July 1, 1983. Social Security checks would have to be held up until additional taxes could be collected, and that could take weeks, during which the elderly, many of whom depend on those checks for most or all of their income, would fall behind in paying rent, food and fuel bills.

That dismal prospect was central to a political drama that began . . . [in May 1982]. Senate Republican leaders met with Administration officials to cobble together some kind of budget for fiscal 1983 that would produce overall federal deficits less gaping than those foreseeable under President Reagan's initial proposals. They agreed on a resolution calling for, among other things, $40 billion in "savings" to be taken out of the $568 billion in Social Security expenditures now expected over the next three fiscal years. The $40 billion represents about the amount by which Social Security benefit payments are expected to exceed tax collections, but the resolution designedly gave no hint as to whether the savings would be accomplished by reducing future benefits, raising taxes, or whatever. Chairman Pete Domenici of New Mexico got the Budget Committee in the Republican-controlled Senate to approve the plan on a partisan 11-to-9 vote.

Democrats, who view Social Security as one of the New Deal's proudest achievements, howled that the Republicans were trying "to balance the budget on the backs of old people." The Budget Committee in the Democrat-controlled House . . . passed a competing resolution to trim federal deficits primarily by reducing military spending and raising non–Social Security taxes; it said nothing at all about Social Security cuts. Only eleven of the 54 G.O.P. Senators are up for re-election this fall. But every member of the House, Republican as well as Democrat, faces the potential wrath of elderly voters worried about a cut in their benefits. Rebelling against the $40 billion proposal, House Republican Leader Robert Michel of Illinois warned, "You've got to take that off the table before you even start" drafting a budget.

Caught in the crossfire, Reagan artfully dodged the matter at his press conference. . . . [May 20] He said, "The Social Security issue is obscuring the main problem, which is: pass the budget." He assured the elderly that they would go on receiving their present pensions, plus a 7.4 percent cost of living increase due July 1. Any future changes, he asserted, would have to await the year-end report of a bipartisan commission headed by Economist Alan Greenspan, which he and Congress appointed last December in a transparent effort to defer the issue until after the November congressional elections. The President did concede that there are times when "you could temporarily put a ceiling on a cost of living adjustment," which he correctly pointed out would not be a cutback but simply a reduction in the amount of increase.

In short, the outlook is for more wrangling and no action on Social Security, at least until after a bitter congressional election campaign in which Democratic candidates will portray themselves as saving the system from Republican assaults and many G.O.P. opponents will undoubtedly pledge undying fealty to Social Security.

Reforming the system, however, cannot be evaded, even though the day of reckoning—when Social Security runs out of money—can and probably will be postponed. One way: allow the retirement fund to continue borrowing from the separate disability and Medicare funds, as it is doing this year. But the three funds could all too easily run dry during 1984; not only pension checks but disability payments and Medicare reimbursements to hospitals that care for the aged sick

would be delayed. At very best, the system will barely squeak
through the 1980s, in constant danger of running short of
funds. That narrow escape will occur only if the economy
booms, thus raising tax collections more than anyone dares to
predict. Even then, Social Security faces a long-range crisis in
the early 21st century as fewer and fewer working people
have to support more and more elderly.

Politicians have made several attempts to solve the problem, but nothing has worked. Social Security beneficiaries
oppose with passion and fury any notion that they should not
get at least inflation-matching increases, and they are likely to
exact speedy revenge at the polls. Their concern is currently
being fed by the prospect that they may be made scapegoats
for a financial mess created primarily by the overly generous
$750 billion tax cut passed by Congress last year at Reagan's
insistence. In fact, Social Security is an obvious target for anyone seeking to hold down federal spending, and thus the
deficit, simply because the program is so enormous. Social
Security benefit payments have rocketed from $33.8 bil-
lion in fiscal 1970 to an estimated $206.5 billion (including
Medicare) in the fiscal year starting next October 1.
This total amounts to 26 percent of all anticipated federal
expenditures.

More fundamentally, the aged have been misled for two
generations into believing that Social Security payments constitute no more than a return to them of the payroll taxes that
they have paid during their working years. This is dramatically untrue. The average retired person today can expect to
collect lifetime benefits five times as great as the total taxes
that he or she once paid: plus interest. From the very first
(Social Security check No. 1, for $22.54, went in January 1940
to Ida Fuller of Brattleboro, Vt., who had paid a total of $22
in Social Security taxes. Fuller drew her last monthly check,
for $112.60, in December 1974, shortly after her 100th birth-
day. By then she had collected $20,944.42 in return for her
$22), Social Security benefits have been paid out of taxes de-
ducted from the paychecks of people working that year, who

in turn have to rely at their retirement on benefits from taxes paid by their children's generation.

Background

No matter: the elderly, and many of the young, have been convinced that they have a right to Social Security payments high enough to maintain a comfortable standard of living despite old age, widowhood or disability, and this right is every bit as inalienable as the rights to life, liberty and the pursuit of happiness. Harold Sheppard, associate director of the National Council on the Aging, has a one-word description of benefits paid now and all increases that may be necessary to keep those payments abreast of inflation. The word is: sacred. And all politicians know that the aged are far more likely to vote than the young.

At bottom, the Social Security system and the nation face a crisis of political leadership. The aged, the widowed, the disabled and even the young have been promised more than the nation can guarantee to deliver at any reasonable cost. Leaders must explain why those promises are getting harder and harder to keep. The answers begin a long way back.

The idea that national governments, rather than churches, charities or extended families, might have to concern themselves with helping the old and the disabled is relatively new in history. Imperial Germany in 1889 enacted the first pension plan, financed by equal contributions from employers and employees, largely because Chancellor Otto von Bismarck saw it as a method to wean the masses away from socialism. As he explained candidly: "Whoever has a pension for his old age is far more content and far easier to handle than one who has no such prospect." Similar plans were adopted by most other major industrial nations over the next three decades.

But the U.S. sticking by its tradition of rugged individualism, held out. Theodore Roosevelt ran for President in 1912 on a Progressive Party platform calling for a national system of social insurance. He lost, and the proposal was not an issue again in presidential elections until 1932, when another Roosevelt, Franklin, campaigned for the White House in a Depression-ravaged nation where the plight of the elderly had become desperate.

Even after Roosevelt's landslide victory, Congress was reluctant to enact a plan that seemed far too radical to some members. Roosevelt repeatedly warned congressional leaders that if they did not approve a moderate Social Security bill, popular pressure would force them to adopt irresponsible Government handout schemes like the ones being pushed by California's Dr. Francis Townsend and Louisiana Governor Huey Long. To soothe conservative qualms, Roosevelt demanded that his planners draft a scheme that was not "the same old dole." That ruled out any use of general revenues, meaning primarily income taxes, to finance any part of Social Security. The system had to be funded entirely by a payroll tax levied half on employers and half on workers, so that it could be presented to the nation as a sort of contributory insurance plan. To this day, paycheck stubs identify Social Security taxes withheld from a worker's wages as FICA—for Federal Insurance Contributions Act—deductions.

The retirement program set up by the Social Security Act of 1935 was modest. It covered workers in commerce and industry only (leaving out the self-employed, farmers, service workers and government employees), plus their spouses and dependents. Taxes, collected beginning in 1937, were set at 1 percent of the first $3,000 of a worker's pay, a maximum of $30 a year, with a matching levy on the employer. Benefits initially averaged $22.60 a month. Those were moderate sums even then, and designedly so. Social Security, as Roosevelt made quite clear, was not intended to guarantee a comfortable retirement; it was meant to ward off destitution. Said F.D.R. while signing the law: "We can never insure 100 percent of the population against 100 percent of the hazards and vicissitudes of life, but we have tried to frame a law which will give some measure of protection to the average citizen and to his family . . . against poverty-ridden old age." It was a point that his political successors would have done well to remember, and most certainly did not.

Congress began trying to provide old-age insurance for something close to 100 percent of the population as early as 1939, before the first Social Security benefits were paid. It decreed that if a pensioner died, benefits would continue to be paid to the widow and dependents. Since then, coverage has been steadily expanded to include farm and domestic workers; employees of state and local governments and non-profit organizations like hospitals; self-employed people, including doctors and lawyers; members of the armed forces; even ministers and members of religious orders, so long as they do not take vows of poverty. Retired millionaires collect, as well as laborers; benefits go to almost anyone who has ever paid Social Security taxes and to some people who never have. In recognition of their important role in society, housewives who have not worked outside the home and thus never paid into the system collect benefits equal to 50 percent of those earned by their husbands.

In time, whole new programs were added. In 1956 Congress started payments, financed by Social Security taxes, to disabled workers, and in later years it greatly liberalized the definitions of who could qualify. Though the eligibility rules were tightened last year at Reagan's request, the program costs $17.7 billion a year. In 1965 the Medicare program was enacted to help cover the hospital and medical bills of people 65 or older. Hospital bills are paid out of a portion of Social Security taxes assigned to a separate trust fund; insurance to pay doctors' bills is financed by voluntary contributions from the elderly who elect to sign up. Current cost of the compulsory Medicare program to Social Security: $34 billion annually.

An especially important expansion began in 1956, when Congress permitted women to retire at 62 rather than 65, on 80 percent of the standard pension; men were allowed to do the same in 1961. Today two-thirds of all Social Security pensioners retire before the "normal" age of 65. Although their pensions are lower, they not only collect benefits for more

years, they also pay taxes into the system for fewer years.
When Social Security began, only 54 percent of all men and
62 percent of all women lived until 65; those who did make it
that far could expect to live another 12.8 years. By 1980,
68 percent of all men and 82 percent of all women could expect to live until 65, and those who reach that age this year
will, on average, live—and collect pensions—for more than
16 years.

Besides making ever more people eligible for benefits,
Congress, with the approval of the White House, kept raising
the payments—eleven times between 1950 and 1972, six of
those times during election years. It seemed a safe as well as a
wonderfully popular thing for politicians to do; into the early
1970s, tax collections almost without exception ran ahead of
benefit payments, and the Social Security trust funds ran sur-
pluses.

In 1972 a fateful moment came. Arkansas Democrat Wilbur Mills, chairman of the House Ways and Means Committee, was in the middle of what turned out to be a brief and
futile run for the Democratic presidential nomination. Mills
pushed through Congress a bill raising Social Security benefits 20 percent. More important, the bill decreed that beginning in 1975, Social Security benefits were to be keyed to the
Consumer Price Index. If the CPI in the first quarter of any
year averages more than 3 percent higher than it was twelve
months earlier, benefits are raised the following July by an
amount equal to the full increase.

As a method of protecting the incomes of the aged against
inflation, the move was questionable to begin with. The CPI is
heavily influenced by increases in housing prices and mortgage interest rates, but relatively few of the elderly buy
houses. In any case, the increases were spectacularly mis-
timed. From 1975 through 1981, the CPI shot up at some of
the fastest inflationary rates in American history. Social Security benefits more than kept pace. The maximum annual benefit jumped 200 percent during the 1970s and has risen 38.5
percent in the past four years. Although inflation is now cool-
ing, benefits are still being boosted to make up for past price

rises. The 7.4 percent increase due July 1 was dictated by inflation that occurred mostly in 1981. When it goes into effect, monthly checks will average $406 for a single pensioner and $695 for a retired couple; the maximum for a single pensioner will be $729.

Such increases have transformed the Social Security system into exactly what Franklin Roosevelt never intended it to be: the primary source of income for most of the aged. In the early years, Social Security pensions averaged 30 percent to 34 percent of a retired person's last monthly paycheck; in 1981 the average was 55 percent. This is the result not only of indexing benefits to the CPI but of generous formulas for calculating initial benefits, which have been written into the law. Only about 30 percent of all Social Security beneficiaries receive private pensions, and various surveys indicate that about one-quarter of the retired depend on Social Security checks for 90 percent of their income. As many as 16 percent are believed to have no other income at all.

Thanks largely to Social Security, the rate of poverty among the elderly has dropped from 29.5 percent in 1967 to 15.7 percent in 1980. Says M.I.T. Economist Lester Thurow: "Social Security was a system designed to move us toward a world where the elderly were treated equally with the non-elderly. We have virtually reached that world."

But as Thurow and many others also emphatically point out, continuing to raise Social Security benefits may soon make the elderly better off than the young, whose earnings are not protected against inflation. And the costs are staggering. In 1975—by no coincidence the first year that benefits were indexed to inflation—Social Security's pension fund, whose formal title is Old-Age and Survivors Insurance (OASI), paid out more than it took in. By 1977 the drain had become so great as to threaten the financial solvency of the system. This occurred even though taxes had been steadily raised from that original $30 a year. By the mid-'70s the maximum amount paid by any worker had reached $825.

Congress responded in 1977 by passing an act calculated to raise $227 billion in additional Social Security taxes during

the following ten years—on top of substantial increases that
had already been written into law. The maximum tax will rise
from $965 in 1977 to at least $3,025 in 1987, because tax rates
rise steadily and the proportion of earnings to which they
apply goes up every year. The maximum Social Security tax
this year has hit $2,170—6.7 percent of earnings up to
$32,400—an increase of 125 percent in just five years. The
taxes are a serious burden on the economy; it is estimated that
about one-quarter of all American families pay more in Social
Security taxes than they do in income taxes. In theory, employers pay a tax exactly as heavy as that levied on their
workers. Actually, many economists believe that the employer's share of the tax is in effect paid by workers and consumers. If an employers' Social Security contribution rises, as
it does now every year, he will either pass out smaller raises to
his workers or increase the price of his products, or both. Alternatively, he may decide to hire fewer workers. Thus the
Social Security tax is believed to increase both inflation and
unemployment.

When the 1977 payroll-tax increase passed Congress, leg-
islators congratulated themselves on having assured the financial solvency of Social Security for the next 50 years. Alas,
they did not ensure it for four years. Benefits kept being
pushed up by inflation. Tax collections, despite the sharp increases in rates, were held down by recessions and wide-
spread unemployment, which in April hit a post–World War
II high of 9.4 percent of the labor force. The impact on the
Social Security system of a 1 percent rise in unemployment is
far greater than that of a 1 percent increase in the inflation
rate. Every time one U.S. worker is laid off, the system loses
more than $125 a month in taxes that he and his employer no
longer pay.

By last year, the OASI fund was perilously close to running out of money. After his May 1981 recommendations
were rejected, President Reagan proposed a makeshift bar-
gain: the Greenspan commission would be appointed to recommend what ought to be done by December 31, 1982, and,

to keep the fund from running dry before then, Social Security should be given permission to borrow from the disability and Medicare funds. Congress granted that permission, but only for 1982.

That was scarcely a stopgap solution. If the borrowing authority is allowed to lapse and the retirement fund goes back on its own on January 1, the fund will be able to send out checks on time only through June 1983. Extending the permission for OASI to borrow from the disability and Medicare funds would buy a bit of additional time, but probably no more than 18 months.

The three funds together took in $178.2 billion in 1981, or $3.1 billion more than they paid out during the period. Defenders of Social Security benefits sometimes cite this surplus as proof that there is no crisis. But Social Security's trustees (Secretary of the Treasury Donald Regan, Secretary of Labor Raymond Donovan and Secretary of Health and Human Services Richard Schweiker) have warned that the disability and Medicare fund reserves are too low to guarantee the timely payment of benefits beyond "sometime during 1984," unless the system is reformed. And if the economy grows vigorously from now through the rest of the 1980s—a fiscal event very few economists are predicting—the funds will barely squeeze by, with no margin to guard against a temporary downturn.

THE GROWING SOCIAL SECURITY SYSTEM[3]

On the third day of each month some 35 million green U.S. Government checks are delivered to homes or deposited directly in banks across the nation. The checks, which averaged just under $300 each in 1979, represent the monthly installment in the country's largest system of transfer pay-

[3] From magazine article entitled "The Social Security System," by Eli Ginzburg, sociologist. *Scientific American.* 246:51–4. Ja. '82. Reprinted with permission. Copyright © 1982 by Scientific American, Inc. All rights reserved.

ments: the Social Security system. The total benefits paid out
in 1979 to 22 million retired or disabled workers and 13 million dependents and survivors came to more than $104 bil-
lion. Unlike a funded pension system, in which contributions
to the system are invested to pay future beneficiaries, Social
Security is founded on a pay-as-you-go approach. This means
that the taxes employees and employers pay into the system
provide the funds to cover current payments to beneficiaries.
These payments amount to more than 6 percent of the total
disposable income of individuals in the U.S.

Transfers of income through the Social Security system
fulfill an implicit contract between younger people currently
in the active work force and people no longer working. This
intergenerational compact has been in effect since 1940,
when the first person to qualify for Social Security benefits
retired. Now the financial soundness of the contract is in
question. Indeed, for much of last year the country was given
to believe the Social Security system faced imminent bankruptcy. It did not, but in the absence of remedial actions
taken by Congress in the fall it would have developed a serious cash-flow problem in the next year or so. Nevertheless,
the cash-flow problem was a manifestation of an underlying
imbalance between revenues and expenditures. The success
of the remedy for the immediate difficulty should not divert
attention from the root causes of the imbalance and the long-
term need for a thorough reform of the system.

The sources of the difficulties can readily be identified.
Since Social Security is a pay-as-you-go system, the taxes paid
by employees and employers in, say, 1950 provided the cash
for 1950's disbursements to beneficiaries, and this year's tax
receipts will pay this year's benefits. Such a system is at the
mercy of economic and demographic forces. For a long time
those forces worked to the advantage of the system. As the
U.S. economy expanded, employment increased and wages at
least kept up with inflation; a high birthrate (which peaked
during the baby boom of the 1950s) and a rise in women's employment brought into the labor force many more new work-

ers than were lost through retirement. As a result income from payroll taxes exceeded benefit payments.

Now all of that is changing. Wages (which, together with the level of employment and the tax rate, determine payroll-tax receipts) have been lagging behind inflation while benefits (which are price-indexed) are protected, even overprotected. What is more important in the long run, lower fertility and greater longevity are changing the age structure of the U.S. population, increasing the number of potential beneficiaries faster than the number of workers who will be asked to support them. An 18-year-old who enters covered employment today is not scheduled to retire until the decade of the 2020s; the system may have to provide benefits for him and his survivors until the 2040s. As one analyst put it, 85 percent of those who will receive benefits in the next 75 years are alive today; 96 percent of all Social Security benefits to be paid during the next 75 years will go to people who are alive today; 99 percent of the payroll taxes to be paid in the next 25 years and 81 percent of the taxes to be paid in the next 50 years will be paid by people alive today.

Congress has no option but to consider how it is going to cover the liabilities it is assuming today. Before the year 2010 the baby-boom cohorts will begin to retire. We therefore have some 30 years in which to restructure the Social Security system.

The U.S. came late to the idea that people should look to the central government to protect an individual against the loss of income as a result of age or disability and to provide for his dependents in the event of his death. Germany had established a government-sponsored pension program in 1889, the U.K. in 1908 and France in 1910. The Social Security Act was passed in 1935, in the heyday of the New Deal. President Roosevelt decided (over the objections of some advisers) to limit coverage at first to workers in industry and commerce and to limit their benefits to cash payments after they stopped working at the age of 65, a retirement age chosen with less than full deliberation. It was generally understood, however, that the system would subsequently be broadened. Even before the first benefit checks were issued Congress amended the law to provide benefits for the aged wife and the children of a retired worker and to the widow and young children of a covered worker on his death.

Two major programs were grafted onto the original system. In 1956 disability insurance was added for covered workers who become unable to work because of sickness or injury. In 1965 Medicare was added. It has two components: hospital insurance and supplementary medical insurance, which help patients to cover physician's charges. The original nucleus of the Social Security system is formally called Old Age and Survivors' Insurance (OASI). When disability insurance is included, the program is designated OASDI, and with hospital insurance OASDHI. All these programs are financed by payroll taxes. Supplementary medical insurance is funded separately. It is an optional program, although most Medicare beneficiaries elect to participate in it; premiums paid by the beneficiaries now cover 30 percent of the cost and the remainder is paid from the general revenues of the federal government.

About 90 percent of all currently employed people are covered by the system. They are subject to a payroll tax (now 6.7 percent of their wages up to $32,400), which is matched by a tax paid by employers. A large proportion of the more than eight million self-employed people are covered; they pay 75 percent of the combined employee-employer rate. The largest category of people not covered by Social Security are government employees, for whom there are 68 federal retirement plans and thousands of other plans for employees of state and local governments. Workers in some nonprofit institutions are also not covered.

From its inception the Social Security system was designed to meet two conflicting objectives. The basic intention was to establish a compulsory system of mandated contributions that would provide income after retirement. In keeping with a national predilection for "paying one's own way" and to gain broad public support, the benefits were to be related to the amount of "contributions." The more tax money that was paid by a worker, the higher his benefits would be at retirement.

Another intention, however, was to ensure that even people who had earned low wages would have enough income in old age to meet their basic needs. That could not be accomplished if benefits were directly proportional to tax payments; the benefit-to-tax ratio had to be skewed in favor of low-wage earners. Today the average unmarried male worker who retired in 1979 after having earned wages at the maximum taxable level will have received by the time of his death 4.97 times as much in benefits as he paid in taxes; the ratio of total benefits to total taxes for an unmarried low earner is 7.07 for men and 8.82 for women. For a retired person with a dependent spouse the benefit-to-tax ratio rises to 9.19 for a maximum earner and 13.06 for a minimum earner. What has made such high ratios possible, of course, is the pay-as-you-go scheme, combined with the economic and demographic forces I mentioned above. (It is often pointed out, incidentally, that the Social Security tax is regressive: not only is the tax rate the same at all income levels but also the fraction of the income on which the tax is paid is larger for a low earner than it is for a high earner. On the benefit side, however, the system is clearly progressive: it favors low earners.)

A retiring worker's benefit is based on his earnings in jobs subject to the payroll tax, except that for years when the earnings were higher than the maximum amount taxed, only that maximum is included. To calculate the benefit the earnings are first adjusted for the increase in wage levels since the money was earned. After a certain number of lowest-pay years are excluded the wage-indexed annual earnings up to age 62 for retiring workers are divided by 12 and averaged. Then a benefit formula is applied to the average indexed monthly earnings to determine the "primary insurance amount" (PIA). The formula is complex, but in essence what it does is convert successively higher increments of earnings into the PIA at successively lower percentages. Thus the benefit for a low-wage worker is a larger percentage of his average wage than the benefit for a high-income worker is. That overall percentage is called the replacement rate. It ranges from almost 70 percent for the lowest-wage earners to about 33 percent for someone who has earned the maximum taxable wage each year; the average replacement rate is 40 to 50 percent. The PIA is the benefit for a retired 65-year-old worker without dependents. It is adjusted if he retires before or after 65 or if he has a spouse or dependent children.

To the extent that Social Security is considered a social insurance plan, people who contribute to it are entitled to draw benefits. The concept of entitlement has protected Social Security from political attack (as President Roosevelt foresaw it would); it has also discouraged any reduction in benefits once they are granted. (It seems to me, however, that the high ratio of benefits to tax payments argues against the idea that any reduction in benefits would constitute a breach of faith with those who have been paying the tax, particularly if the adjustment is made after due warning.)

The concept of the system as contributory insurance has been reinforced by the decision to rely exclusively on the payroll tax as the source of revenue to pay OASDHI benefits. Most of the planners of the system assumed that in time there would be partial recourse to general revenues. They had in mind an eventual three-way division, characteristic of most European pension systems, in which employees, employers and the central government each contribute a third of the necessary funds. The direct linkage between taxes and benefits has helped Congress resist pressure to raise benefits without consideration of how they would be financed.

Social Security cannot be discussed without attention to other measures intended to provide income maintenance. The same motives that led the federal government to pass the Social Security Act led to the establishment of various programs providing cash or other benefits for people whose income is too low to meet their basic needs. Whereas Social Security benefits are paid regardless of need to all qualified workers whose earnings have been taxed, most other public programs are means-tested: benefits go only to those who have a demonstrated need.

The means-tested programs began modestly in the 1930s when the federal government joined with the states to give aid to families with dependent children (AFDC), which still accounts for the bulk of what is referred to as welfare payments. Assistance was also provided for the blind and later for disabled and needy old people excluded from or not adequately supported by Social Security; in the early 1970s the federal government assumed responsibility for these groups with the Supplemental Security Income program. In 1965 the joint federal-state Medicaid program was established for people on welfare and for others defined by each state as medically needy. Other in-kind programs aim to provide adequate nutrition (food stamps and other assistance) and housing (rent subsidies) for low-income people. In 1979 the total federal outlay for means-tested programs was $35 billion, compared with the total outlay for OASDI of $104 billion.

In spite of the country's commitment to rely on social insurance to cover the basic needs of those unable to work because of age or disability, more than two million OASDI recipients in 1979 needed supplemental income. When all income from all sources, including Social Security and means-tested programs, cash as well as in-kind, are taken into account, no more than 3 or 4 percent of the elderly fall below the poverty line. About a third of the elderly, however, are not much above that line. Of course, Social Security benefits were never meant to be the sole source of income for older people. Most aged families with a satisfactory standard of living receive less than half of their income from OASDI benefits; they rely also, in different proportions at different income levels, on continued earnings by family members, on savings and on private pensions.

Private pension systems antedated the establishment of Social Security, although they became a significant factor only during and after World War II. Between 1950 and 1975 the number of workers covered by private plans grew from

9.8 to 30.3 million, the number of monthly beneficiaries from 450,000 to more than seven million and annual benefit payments from \$370 million to \$14.8 billion. In 1979 almost two-thirds of all male workers and half of all female workers were covered by a private plan. Nevertheless, in 1980 such plans accounted for only 14 percent of all retirement, disability and survivors' benefits; 78 percent came from Social Security and other federal retirement systems and 8 percent came from state and local systems.

The fundamental importance of the Social Security system is clear. It has often been stated (and it is probably true) that the system is the government's most successful social program. It is all the more imperative, then, that the system be kept financially sound.

The cash-flow crisis that was imminent last fall affected only one part of the OASDHI system. Under current law benefits for each Social Security program can be paid only from the specific trust fund for that program. It is the OASI fund that is in trouble. At the beginning of 1960 the money in that fund amounted to 195 percent of the total outlay for 1960; last October 1 (at the beginning of the 1982 fiscal year) the balance was down to 14 percent of the estimated expenditure for 1982. The Congressional Budget Office has a rule of thumb: the starting balance each year must be at least 9 percent of the year's expected outlay in order to cover benefits paid early in the fiscal year, before current payroll-tax money is collected. In the absence of congressional action the OASI balance would have fallen to less than 5 percent by next October.

The primary cause of the decline in the trust-fund balances in the 1970s was a series of three large increases in benefits: 15 percent in 1970, 10 percent in 1971 and 20 percent in 1972. In addition in 1972 the escalation of benefits was institutionalized: Congress decided that benefits should routinely be raised to match any increase of more than 3 percent per year in the Consumer Price Index. As a result benefits have been raised every year since 1975. The increases were to be financed by raising the taxable wage base as current average wages rose. Prices outstripped wages, however; indexed benefits rose faster than the indexed wage base.

Faced with the combined effects of benefit increases, high unemployment and slow economic growth, Congress (having no inclination to alter reliance on the payroll tax and being loath to reduce benefits) enacted a series of increases in the total OASDHI tax rate in 1977. In conjunction with the rising tax base the rate increases were expected to ensure the financial stability of the system for the remainder of the century. It was not enough. Less than three years later Congress had to transfer some tax receipts from the disability-insurance fund to OASI. Then last fall it had to take emergency action again, diverting some future tax receipts from the disability and hospital-insurance funds to OASI and also allowing for the possibility of interfund borrowing. According to projections made by the Congressional Budget Office, however, neither interfund borrowing nor even a complete merger of the trust funds will sustain the system for long. By the beginning of fiscal year 1985 the combined balance for all three funds will fall below 9 percent of expected expenditures.

What then? February [1981], the Congressional Budget Office identified a number of alternatives that in various combinations could carry the system through the 1980s. For example, many economists now think cost-of-living increases tend to overcompensate for inflation and that they could be modified. The minimum benefit, which increases the payment that would otherwise be received by certain very low earners, could be eliminated. Congress has already eliminated the "lump sum" death benefit and special benefits for dependent students.

The Budget Office has also suggested a number of ways to increase revenue, such as allowing the system to borrow from the U.S. Treasury, accelerating scheduled tax increases, raising the tax base to include all earnings and raising the self-employment tax. Hospital benefits might be paid in full or in part with money from specifically earmarked income-tax receipts so that the hospital-care payroll tax could be allocated to OASDI. Congress could consider forgoing some future income-tax cuts and instead allocating some portion of any proposed cut to the Social Security trust funds. Others have suggested that half of each benefit payment should be subject to the income tax: the half financed by employers' contributions, on which no tax was ever paid. Although beneficiaries with low incomes would not pay the tax, the yield would still be about $4.5 billion per year.

Given all these options, it seems most unlikely that the system will fail to meet its obligations in the next few years. Combined with the action already taken by Congress, adding only .5 percent to the total payroll tax rate would right the balance between revenues and expenditures unless the economy goes into a long decline. . . .

THE SHOCKING SHAPE OF THINGS TO COME[4]

As it stands today, Social Security is simply an income transference scheme. A payroll tax is levied, taking money away from workers and their employers, and the proceeds are given to Social Security beneficiaries. Nearly all of the proceeds are consumed. Nothing is invested.

To understand why this can't go on indefinitely we have to understand what productive investment really is. Under a private financial system productive people who are currently producing more than they need or desire to consume, and who wish to provide for their future needs, transfer purchasing power through time. They usually do that by making deposits with financial institutions—banks, life insurance companies and the like—that pay a rent, called interest, for the use of their savings, and repay the principal whenever the savers need or desire to spend their savings.

For its part, the private financial system transfers purchasing power from the savers, who are currently producing more than they need or wish to spend, to the investors who

[4] Excerpt from magazine article by Ashby Bladen, insurance executive. *Forbes.* 125:39–40. My. 26, '80. Copyright 1980 by Forbes Magazine. Reprinted by permission.

have an opportunity to buy and put to profitable use the capital goods—such as tools, factories, trucks and bridges—that make human efforts more efficient and productive. It is the increased productivity that these capital goods provide that makes it possible for investors to pay savers a rent for the use of their savings.

All this is elementary economics, but that's my point. Our present Social Security system ignores basic economics. The main shortcoming of the Social Security system is that it accomplishes neither of the desirable transfers of purchasing power that we just discussed. Since it is financed by a payroll tax upon current productive efforts, it does not transfer purchasing power through time, nor does it accumulate savings that can be used to finance productive real investments. What it *does* do is supplant much of the savings that people would otherwise make in order to provide for their own future needs and responsibilities. No significant amount of financial or real assets have been accumulated to make good on the Social Security system's promises. Nevertheless, as long as you believe that the promises will be kept, it makes sense to reduce proportionately the savings that you would otherwise make for your old age and enjoy the good things of life now. Martin Feldstein has estimated that the existence of the pay-as-you-go Social Security system has reduced our national savings rate by about 50 percent and is thus largely responsible for our appallingly low level of real investment that is causing our economy to become uncompetitive with countries like Germany and Japan, where the personal savings rate, as a percent of income, is several times higher than it is here. Indeed, when we take account of the fact that the historical-cost basis of depreciating capital assets falls far short of providing their replacement costs in an era of severe inflation, the U.S. on balance is probably consuming capital. Like Great Britain, we are living off past savings.

The amount of savings that the Social Security system has displaced is not peanuts. If a private financial institution, like a life insurance company, had made the promises that Social Security has made, it would have accumulated a fund out of

savings that would be $2 trillion to $4 trillion larger than the
assets of the Social Security system. A full year's national income is about $2 trillion. If we had made anything like that
much additional investment in productive facilities during
the last 45 years, our national standard of living would probably not be falling today.

The final problem with Social Security is not a fundamental one but rather a fact of political life. When a mutual life
insurance company like the one I work for makes a promise of
benefits in the future, it assumes that just about everything
that could go wrong will, and it charges a premium that will
almost certainly be more than adequate. Then, as time reveals how much of the premium was unnecessary, the excess
is refunded as a policyholder's dividend, while the basic premium remains adequate to provide the promised benefit
under almost any conceivable circumstances.

Politicians, on the other hand, set payroll taxes at the
lowest level they think they can get away with if nothing
much does go wrong. And they have yet to grapple with the
fact that the American people had a lot of children after
World War II who will be ready to retire in the early 2000s
and seem to have chosen fun and careers rather than children.
So by the turn of the century there will be relatively fewer
working people to pay the Social Security taxes and support
the retirees. During the rest of this century, it is estimated
there will be about five workers supporting each retired person, and the Social Security system will continue to work. By
the year 2025 the ratio will be about 3-to-1, and it's virtually
impossible that the present system will continue to work.

Last year the payroll tax rate for all the Social Security
programs was 6.13 percent of covered payrolls for both employer and employee, or 12.56 percent in total. It is scheduled
to rise to 15.30 percent in 1990 and remain there in subsequent years. But A. Haeworth Robertson, who was chief actuary of the Social Security Administration until 1978, has estimated that it will, in fact, have to rise to at least 24 percent
by the year 2025. That, I submit, is much too high. Long before we reach that point a great many people will have

ceased to work at all, or will have moved into the subterranean economy. And since what counts is the total tax burden, shifting some of it from the payroll tax to the income tax would not alter the fundamental situation in any appreciable way.

To sum up: The real purpose of productive investment is to transfer purchasing power through time, to postpone consumption today to make possible greater production in the future. Social Security as practiced in this country now is an attempt both to eat the cake and to have it later. Even a child can see that won't work. Unless we can find ways to make Social Security more than a mere scheme for the transfer of consumption from one group to another and transform it into a true savings program, we are building up a mess for the future that may make inflation and the energy crisis look like a piece of pie.

Paying the Social Security benefits will not become an acute problem until the early years of the next century; but financing Social Security out of taxes upon current productive efforts—instead of by savings—is already having a significant impact upon the American standard of living. Sometime, somehow and fairly soon, Social Security is simply going to have to be financed just like private pensions, through saving and productive investment; or else our standard of living will really go to pot and Social Security benefits will ultimately prove to be unsustainable. . . .

II. THE PROBLEMS

EDITOR'S INTRODUCTION

President Roosevelt's and Treasury Secretary Morgenthau's fearful predictions in 1935 of building "up an accumulated deficit for the Congress of the United States to meet in 1980" were bound to come true (see Schlesinger excerpt in Section I). The articles in this section bear out the President's words.

The percentage of elderly in the population of the United States is increasing at an alarming rate for our Social Security system and it will gradually peak when the post World War II babies become senior citizens in the years 2000 to 2025. Such projections and their implications for Social Security are examined and explained in a clear and concise study by Harrison Donnelly. Reprinted from the *Congressional Quarterly*, this study introduces the section.

The impact of these demographic considerations is also discussed by A. F. Erhbar in an excerpt from his article in *Fortune*. He looks at the enormous projected payroll tax rate which will be needed when the baby boomers retire. In this connection, former Secretary of Commerce, Peter Peterson, declares in a quote from his article in the *New York Times Magazine* (Ja. 17, '82), "The young worker starting his payroll contributions today will be very fortunate if he receives benefits merely equal to what he pays in."

In a candid reassessment of Social Security ills and its imminent bankruptcy in the *Journal of the Institute of Socioeconomic Studies*, Tom Bethell points out in the third article that the present structure of the Social Security system and its provisions for early retirement serve as disincentives for capable older people who can work. He feels that raising the retirement age would help the system financially and benefit the retirees healthwise.

Then, a less pessimistic assessment of the financial health

of Social Security, entitled "The Solvency of the Social Security System," reassures us that "the Social Security System as a whole is relatively sound." The New York State Task Force on Social Security found, however, that the Medicare component in the system will be more of a financial problem in the future.

Along with the problems already discussed, there are other abuses in the Social Security system that are more immediate and more amenable to solution. The fifth article from *U.S. News & World Report*, by James Hildreth, spotlights a number of cases where Social Security's antiquated computers have made serious and costly blunders. This writer and the next one, Nick Thimmesch, are concerned about the prevalence of fraud in the system. In his article in the *Saturday Evening Post*, Thimmesch writes of numerous instances of the public defrauding the Social Security system of billions of dollars by accepting checks made out in error to dead retirees. The Reagan administration is attempting to remedy these situations.

PERCENTAGE OF AGED TO GROW SHARPLY, AS BABY BOOM TURNS GRAY[1]

Today's elderly Americans are doing relatively well, but younger people face an uncertain old age.

Current statistics and future projections by the Census Bureau and the Social Security Administration (SSA) show that federal policies have been largely successful in eliminating grinding poverty among the elderly.

But those policies face severe strains in the future, as the proportion of the U.S. population aged 65 and over grows from the current 11.1 percent to a projected 20.4 percent by 2030—a mere 50 years from now. A relatively small work

[1] Reprint of magazine article by Harrison Donnelly, staff writer. *Congressional Quarterly.* 39:2321+. N. 28, '81. Copyright 1981 Congressional Quarterly Inc. Reprinted by permission.

force will have to find ways, either through government or private efforts, to support a massive dependent group.

The elderly population also will change in ways that could increase demands for government assistance.

More people will reach a very old age—80 and beyond—when health care costs grow enormously. They will be increasingly dependent on social support—for income as well as medical care—as years of retirement consume their savings.

The Aging Today

There were 25,544,133 people age 65 and over in the United States in 1980, according to the Census Bureau. Statistics compiled by Herman B. Brotman, consultant for the Senate Aging Committee, show that people aged 65 and older:

—Are preponderantly in the 65–69 age category (8.8 million), but with a growing number of the "old old," aged 80 and over (5.2 million).

—Are mostly women—about 15 million, compared with 10 million men 65 and over. As people get older, the female-male ratio gets bigger: 131 women for every 100 men at age 65, but 224 women aged 85 and older for each 100 men the same age.

—Look forward, on average, to another 16.3 years of life on turning 65. Women have an added life expectancy of 18.4 years; men have 14 remaining years.

—Have lower incomes than when they were younger, but generally escape dire poverty. The median income of households headed by elderly persons in 1979 was $11,316—53 percent of the $21,201 median income of younger families. Single elderly persons were somewhat worse off, with a median income of $4,653—48 percent of the $9,706 median income of single younger people.

—Retire earlier than in the past. While roughly 9 percent of women 65 and over remain in the work force, about the same as in the past, only 20 percent of men now continue working past 65, compared with the 46 percent who did so in 1950.

—Live more often in small towns and rural areas than younger people. Reversing a previous pattern, however, they also live more often in the suburbs than in the inner cities.

Projections for the Future

Medical advances, the postwar "baby boom" and sharp changes in attitudes toward childbearing in recent decades have all combined to lay the groundwork for an enormous projected increase in the nation's elderly population.

Like a "pig in a python," the baby-boom generation of 1945–1960—which faced crowded schools while young and is experiencing intense competition for jobs as adults—must look forward uneasily to a retirement dependent on a relatively small working population.

Everyone who will be 65 by the middle of the next century has already been born. So, barring some major catastrophe, demographers have a fairly good idea of how many old people to expect by then. Based on the most reliable assumptions, SSA predicts there will be 64,925,000 older Americans in 2030.

The real question for public policy, however, is the size of the older population as a percentage of the total population. The latest SSA estimates show the portion of the total population aged 65 and over—only 4 percent in 1900—will rise steadily to 20.4 percent by 2030.

Those estimates are based on assumptions about two key factors—life expectancy and fertility rates—that will determine the proportion of elderly. Changes in either could increase or reduce the percentage of elderly in the population.

Life Expectancy

The SSA projection and a similar one by the Census Bureau in 1977 assume that there will be no medical breakthroughs leading to dramatic increases in life expectancy.

Demographers, such as Leon F. Bouvier of the University of Rhode Island, generally assign a relatively small role to increases in life expectancy in determining the size of the aged population. "Medical progress is not the principal cause of this growth [of the aged population]," Bouvier has written. "Indeed, it has played but an inconsequential role."

Most of the increases in life expectancy during the 20th century—from 47.3 years at birth in 1900 to 73.3 years in 1978—have been due to improvements in combating infant mortality and infectious diseases affecting the young, such as polio, diphtheria, smallpox, measles, tetanus and whooping cough.

The improvement in life expectancy of the aged has been much less. In 1900, the average person at 65 could expect 11.9 more years of life; in 1978 a 65-year-old had 16.1 years remaining—a 35 percent increase, compared with a 55 percent increase in life expectancy at birth.

In the last decade, however, there has been substantial progress in fighting the diseases that kill the aged. "Recently, the death rates for older people from certain major diseases have been decreasing. If that continues, then our projections on the size of the older population may be too low," Brotman said.

Fertility

A much more important factor in determining the future proportion of the elderly within the total population is the fertility rate—the average number of babies that women have during their lifetimes. The children born in the last 25 years of the 20th century are the people who will have to support the baby-boom generation in retirement.

During the first 15 years after World War II, fertility rates were extremely high—3.5 lifetime births per woman in 1955, for example. But changing social norms during the 1970s produced a radical drop in the fertility rate. In 1975 the rate was 1.8—a historically low figure that is well below the 2.1 births needed to sustain the population at a stable size over the long term.

Recent experience suggests, however, that many of the baby-boom women who put off having babies are now having them, and that the fertility rate is on the increase. Indeed, most demographers believe that society will not remain at the very low fertility rate. So the chart is based on the common assumption that fertility rates over the next half-century will be about 2.1.

The wild card in population projections is immigration. Demographers assume 400,000 legal immigrants each year. But they do not include illegal immigrants in their projections.

Dependency Ratio

Tomorrow's demographics seem less ominous in the context of the total "dependency ratio," which compares the combined numbers of people under age 18 and over age 65 with the "productive" part of the population aged 18–64.

Brotman notes that the working-age population must support children as well as the elderly. Census Bureau projections, he said, indicate there probably will be 73.8 dependent people for every 100 workers in 2030. That is well above the 64.2 of 1980, but below the 81.9 of 1960, a year of many children.

However, the young and the old put different burdens on society, and the savings from smaller numbers of children—in education, for example—may not match the added income-support and health care costs of a burgeoning elderly population. Nor are such savings easily transferred from one age group to another.

Women and the 'Old Old'

Three other trends affecting the elderly population are important.

First, the elderly will continue to be mostly women. Older women already outnumber men by 50 percent, and the gap is growing. In 2020, SSA projects, there could be 30.9 million older women and only 21.8 million older men.

Most older women, having outlived their spouses, will be alone. More than 70 percent of elderly men in 2020 will be married, compared with just 39 percent of women.

Second, the older population is itself aging. The "old old"—aged 80 and over—will grow from 22 percent of the aged in 1980 to 29 percent by 2000 and 35.9 percent by 2040, when the baby-boom population will have reached advanced age.

By 2060, there could be 4.2 million people aged 95 and over—a truly phenomenal increase from the 163,000 of that age in 1980.

Finally, current low fertility rates will mean that the baby-boom generation will enter retirement with fewer children than past generations of the elderly have had. So they will not be able to depend as much on their children for income support and long-term care. That will increase the importance of social support, particularly from governments.

This large age cohort, which first asserted itself during the protests of the 1960s, could once again become a militant force pressing its demands on the government.

WHEN BABY-BOOMERS RETIRE[2]

... The immediate financial crunch is a mere inconvenience compared to the one that's coming when the baby-boom generation starts retiring 30 years from now. As the multitudes born in the philoprogenitive years following World War II leave the labor force after 2010, the retired population will mushroom. Meanwhile, the population of revenue-producing workers will stagnate because the baby

[2] Excerpt from magazine article entitled "How to Save Social Security," by A. F. Ehrbar, staff writer. *Fortune.* 102:36. Ag. 25, '80. Excerpted from the August 25 issue of FORTUNE Magazine by special permission. Copyright 1980 Time Inc.

boom was followed by the comparatively barren sixties and seventies. By 2030, when the last of the boomers will be over 65, the combined payroll tax rate needed to finance benefits probably will be at least 25 percent of taxable payroll, and could be as high as 36 percent.

Those estimates, and the ones for 2050 [as charted earlier], are derived from the Social Security Administration's intermediate and pessimistic projections (few rational adults heed the optimistic one). Most of the striking difference between the two estimates reflects different assumptions about future fertility and mortality rates. In the pessimistic estimate, the fertility rate continues to fall, as it has in all industrialized countries for the last 150 years, and life expectancy improves at a rapid pace. Those factors combine to lift the number of beneficiaries per 100 workers from 31 today to 68 in 2030 and 84 in 2050 (the number of persons aged 20 to 64 actually declines after 2010). The intermediate estimate assumes a slower gain in life expectancy and an increase in the fertility rate; the number of beneficiaries per 100 workers reaches 52 in 2030 and remains fairly constant after that.

As with the shorter forecasts, many pension experts believe the intermediate projections are too optimistic. One is Thomas Woodruff, executive director of the President's Commission on Pension Policy, a group studying the effects that the baby boom will have on all retirement systems. Woodruff believes the pessimistic projection is more realistic, though the President's Commission is using the intermediate one so its forecasts will be comparable to those of other researchers.

The problem of paying for the retirement of the baby-boom generation is more urgent than it might appear. The only way to avoid sky-high payroll tax rates is to reduce promised benefits, and that should be done soon if it is to be done at all. Cutting benefits may be politically impossible if we wait until the nineties, when the oldest of the postwar generation will be only ten or 15 years away from collecting them. Moreover, it's questionable whether society should alter long-standing commitments so soon before they come due. Says William Agee, chairman of Bendix Corp. and one of the few businessmen who has made a close study of Social Security: "Procrastinating until the burden forces the breaching of promises will only make the problem worse. Young and old will be pitted against one another in a fearful battle over the remains of a shrinking economy."

SOCIAL SECURITY: PERMIT FOR IDLENESS?[3]

It is customary for liberal writers and publications to preface articles on the Social Security system with hurried genuflection, usually consisting of the observation that it is and always has been our "most successful" social program, or something similar. And, indeed, the Social Security system probably was on the whole successful for the first 40 years of its existence—say from 1937 to 1977. But it much less likely to enjoy a comparable success—and as indulgent a press—in its second 40 years. (It is obviously a difficult matter to evaluate the success or failure of something as complex and far-reaching as Social Security. But clearly it is inadequate to claim it has been a success to date on the grounds that all eligible retirees received a check in the mail as promised. We have to consider what the state of the nation would have been *without* Social Security. To mention just one frequently raised objection, our savings rate, and hence capital available for investment, is far lower today than it would have been without Social Security. For years Americans have been encouraged to believe that they do not have to save much because government checks will come to their rescue at age 65. Is this a "good" system for a nation to adopt? Put that way, the issue of Social Security can clearly be viewed as controversial.)

The reason for this is that Social Security is comparable to a game which is very easy to play at the beginning, but which becomes progressively more complex as time goes on. As sev-

[3] Reprint of magazine article by Tom Bethel, Washington D.C. correspondent, *Harper's* magazine. *Journal of the Institute of Socioeconomic Studies.* VI, 3:40–50. Autumn '81. By permission of the Institute for Socioeconomic Studies. All rights reserved.

eral writers have observed, its probability of providing benefits in the years and decades ahead may not be much better
than the chances of an easy-riches seeker who gets in late on a
chain letter.

The beauty of the Social Security Act, when it was enacted in April 1935 (payments did not begin until 1937), was
that the retirement benefits of a relatively small number of
beneficiaries were financed by a large number of workers.
Thus the Old Age and Survivors Insurance (OASI) trust fund
grew rapidly even though those paying into it were assessed
at a very low rate: 1 percent of the first $3,000 of income from
its inception until 1949. That is, no one had to contribute
more than $30 a year to Social Security. By 1947, there were
as many as 22 workers paying into the system for every one
receiving benefits from it.

Escalation

So the politicians—falsely believing that they had at their
disposal a "free" vote-getting program helping one segment
of the electorate without noticeably irritating the remainder—unwisely elected to expand the system over the years.
First, benefits were extended to a pensioner's dependents and
survivors. Then, in 1956, workers who could qualify as disabled, but who had not yet reached the statutory retirement
age of 65 were included. In 1961, there was a further, crucial
expansion. Thenceforth, men could retire at age 62 and receive a portion of their Social Security benefit. (Today, such
early retirees can receive 80 percent of their benefit at 62.)

By 1965, Congress had extended hospital insurance to the
elderly under Medicare; and at the same time began to adjust
the formula whereby benefits were computed, making them
more generous. In 1972, Congress took the fateful step of allowing automatic indexing of payments to keep pace with the
soaring Consumer Price Index.

System Endangered

Almost immediately thereafter, however, dramatic
changes in the overall economy, and in the age structure of

the population, began to combine with all this generosity in ways that boded ill for the future of Social Security. The system began to feel the effects of something that was rather worse than a "double whammy"; it could even be described as a triple whammy. In the first place, as the system matured, more and more people were reaching the "eligible" age of 65—and even more were reaching the age of 62, of course. Not only were more people reaching the age of 65, but life-span after 65 was increasing. The ultimate dollar liability of the system inevitably increased apace.

Secondly, inflation began to increase rapidly in the 1970s, thus automatically increasing the by-now indexed payment levels. This was combined with a drastic development not predicted by economists. According to the Phillips Curve, inflation was supposed to bring down unemployment. But in the 1970s unemployment began *rising* with inflation. When people are unemployed, they cease paying payroll taxes into the system. At the very same time that outflows were increasing because of inflation and a general "graying" of the population, funding was being constricted by unemployment.

Finally, as if this were not enough, the fertility rate of U.S. women declined from a high of 3.7 (children per woman) in 1957 to about half that level today. One consequence is that a generation from now there will be relatively far fewer workers available to pay for the benefits of the abundant "baby boom" generation when *it* has reached retirement age. The number of workers supporting the retirees has now shrunk to a ratio of about three to one. That will reach two to one sometime in the next century. The "unfunded liability" to current workers and retirees is estimated (by the former chief actuary for the Social Security Administration) to be $5.6 trillion.

Imminent Bankruptcy

In 1982, if the system remains unchanged, the Old Age, Survivors and Disability Insurance fund is expected to take in $155 billion and pay out $167 billion—a shortfall of $12 billion. By 1984, this shortfall is expected to be $21.4 billion. In other words, the system is rapidly going bankrupt. Current reserves are now "almost exhausted," according to David A. Stockman, Director of the Office of Management and Budget. Social Security costs have exceeded revenues each year since 1975.

This, then, is the background against which Health and Human Services Secretary Richard S. Schweiker submitted a plan to the House Ways and Means Committee on May 12th of this year to "keep [the Social Security System] from going broke." Four points in the Schweiker proposals attested a Reagan administration intention of sustaining and, to some degree, even increasing Social Security costs:

We will stand by the traditional retirement age of 65; we will not raise it.

We will not propose raising Social Security taxes for the 114 million working men and women now contributing to the system. In fact, we propose future tax reduction.

We will phase out the retirement earnings test, thus ending the penalty now in law which discourages senior citizens from remaining in the labor force to supplement their Social Security income.

These proposals do not remove from the rolls, or cut benefits for, those currently receiving benefits.

But pointing to the system's looming deficits Schweiker also put forward cost-cutting provisions designed to:

—reduce the welfare-oriented elements which duplicate other programs and which have been introduced over the years into the Social Security system;

—relate disability insurance more closely to a worker's earnings history and medical condition;

—reduce the opportunity for "windfall" benefits which now can mean higher monthly benefit checks to a short-term double-dipper worker than to a low-range earner who has spent a lifetime contributing to the system;

—do more to encourage workers to stay on the job until the traditional Social Security retirement age of 65;

—restrain the benefit growth for future retirees by altering temporarily the initial benefit formula computation which takes into account the prior over-indexing in the system.

Necessity of Reform

Defending the rationale on which the intended reform was based, OMB Director Stockman told the House Ways and Means Committee: ". . . critics do not fully understand the magnitude of the crisis facing Social Security. The question is not whether those who seek to retire over the next few years will receive 100, or 80, or 55 percent of what they had previously anticipated. The question before the Congress is whether the 36 million Americans who currently depend on Social Security can count on *any check at all* less than two years hence.

There is one stark and dramatic fact: OASI will bankrupt in *October 1982*. At that point, $14 billion in monthly benefits cannot be paid. Unless a bipartisan consensus can be created, 32 million Americans will not get their checks under current law.

There are four ways in which the Social Security system can be brought under control. The first is the infusion of general revenues into the Social Security trust fund. But the problem here, as Stockman says, is that "the federal government has no uncommitted general revenues for this purpose. General revenues would have to be raised, either as new taxes or new deficit financing, to bail out Social Security." In practice, Stockman suggests, the government would turn to bond financing which "would simply add about $84 billion in *new* red ink to other government financing needs." This in turn would tend to be inflationary, further adding to the underlying structural problem. Moreover, introduction of general revenue financing must cause concern in all quarters. The unfunded liability of Social Security in the years ahead is so enormous that such a proposal could eventually threaten to engulf the federal budget.

A second proposal is to increase Social Security payroll taxes. But it is worth remembering that in 1977 we had the largest peacetime tax increase in U.S. history in order to stave off the insolvency of Social Security. Nonetheless, the reserve ratio of OASDHI continues on its steep downhill path. The new taxes abysmally failed to close the gap between Social Security outlays and revenues.

Perhaps, the new supply-side economists have something to teach us here: attempting to increase tax revenues by increasing tax rates does not seem to work beyond a certain point. To bridge the gap, FICA taxes would have to go up about 25 percent, from a present 13.3 percent of wages, including what is paid by both employee and employer, to more than 16 percent.

A third possibility, frequently mentioned, is "interfund borrowing." The Old Age fund would be enabled to borrow from the Disability Insurance fund, or from the Health Insurance trust fund. The former "would only postpone insolvency for three months, until January 1983," according to Stockman; the latter would give us a lengthier reprieve. But the Health Insurance fund is itself headed for insolvency. Thus, "robbing Peter to pay Paul" would merely jeopardize health insurance benefits for the elderly without solving the fundamental problems which threaten their retirement income. Interfund borrowing would therefore dramatize the system's plight, but not solve it.

Reaction

The reform proposal that attracted the most attention, however, was that urging change of (1) present incentives for early retirement and (2) disincentives for continued employment. The response was almost uniformly hostile. Representative Claude Pepper (D-Fla.), who as chairman of the House Select Committee on Aging has become Congress' leading spokesman on the aged, branded Schweiker's proposal "insidious" and "cruel." To Senator Howard M. Metzenbaum (D-Ohio), the plan constituted a "breach of . . . promise to the elderly." To attempt to lever the reforms with the argument that Social Security is about to go bankrupt amounted to "political terrorism," according to Senator Daniel Patrick Moyn-

ihan (D-N.Y.). Much more significantly, the public perception—as fashioned by television's capsulization and by further transmission by word of mouth—was that the Reagan
proposal was an out-and-out assault on Social Security. What
was elided was the administration's promise of a future decrease in Social Security taxes and the lifting of the penalty
on the earnings of Social Security recipients. Thus, a *Washington Post*/ABC News telephone poll found that 49 percent
of a national sample of adults disapproved of the proposal as
they understood it and by very nearly a two-to-one margin
thought the proposals would be personally harmful to them.

To be sure, some spokesmen not reflexively bound to Reagan were willing to grant good reason for the proposed reform. The *New York Times* editorialized on May 13 [1981]
that "Social Security has become both an inducement for the
productive to leave the work force and an incredibly expensive substitute for personal retirement savings."

Nonetheless, the politically wary immediately perceived
that this was not the time to take a stand for Social Security
reform. The Schweiker proposal had been poorly timed,
rushed to get into the media earlier than a long-promised reform plan from the House Social Security Subcommittee.
Neither White House legislative tacticians nor the Republican leadership of Congress were alerted to Schweiker's time-
table. The entire effort appeared so hopelessly faulty that the
Senate promptly distanced itself from the administration plan
by a crushing 96 to 0 vote.

Such self-righteous exercises as the Senate's 96–0 vote will
not, however, obliterate the problem of early retirement. The
added burdens on non-retired workers of supporting 62-year-
olds who prefer not to work is more than the nation can afford. Nor is the economy capable of foregoing the production
lost by those early retirements.

The Social Security system, as noted by the *New York
Times* editorial writer, creates a strong incentive for people to
retire at age 62. Congressman Sam Gibbons (D-Fla.), the
chairman of the Subcommittee on Oversight of the House
Ways and Means Committee summed up the problem last

year: "The incentives in the Social Security system . . . encourage early retirement to such an extent that today seven out of ten Americans retire before age 65."

By contrast, in 1948 half of all men over 65 were still in the labor force; today fewer than one in five are at work. And since 1961, the proportion of employed men aged 62 to 64 has fallen from eight in ten to less than six in ten.

We have already seen that the main problem with Social Security is that more and more people are becoming eligible for benefits, while relatively fewer are working to pay for those benefits. Yet here we find, as it were at the heart of the system, an incentive structure that tends to take people out of the working population and put them in the recipient population within the very age bracket wherein people are today living longer and with greater health than formerly. Moreover, it is this stratum that has acquired, through a lifetime's experience, valuable skills which could and should be put to use. The fact is that male workers between 55 and 64 constitute one of the most productive work force age groups in the country. [*Time*, Jl. 6, '81] Nonetheless, they have dropped from a labor force participation rate of 85 percent in 1960 to less than 70 percent in 1980.

Encouraging Retirement

Males are now encouraged to retire at age 62 because they can receive 80 percent of their Social Security benefits at this age. Then, after the usual retirement age of 65, an earnings test reduces benefits by 50 cents for every dollar earned over $5,500. But his earnings test is discontinued at age 72.

The dynamic of the incentives encouraging workers to quit eludes some. William C. Hsiao, associate professor of economics at Harvard, contended in testimony before the Ways and Means Subcommittee that many retire early simply because "they prefer leisure over work." It is not surprising. The benefits system is such that the retiree gets paid a substantial part of what he or she would have earned—*without* having to show up for work.

Hsiao also suggests that people prefer to retire early because "the health status of Americans has not improved." It is possible, of course, that early retirement itself undermines health. As for polls showing that people state "health" as a reason for early retirement, this may be construed as the socially acceptable response to pollsters by people who are reluctant to concede that they are, in fact, taking advantage of an unduly generous system.

Jim Storey, director of Income Security and Pension Policy Studies at the Urban Institute, testified at the same hearing: Workers with higher earnings, he said, have a substantial incentive to claim Social Security at age 62 and work part-time up to the cut-off point at which their benefits are penalized because of earnings. "A worker earning $15,000 who retired at age 62 and worked part-time thereafter would have after-tax income worth 83 percent of full-time lifetime earnings."

Special Tax on Working

Richard Burkheiser of Vanderbilt University added trenchantly: "It isn't surprising that older workers react to such powerful anti-work incentives by leaving their jobs. Our Social Security system in effect levies a special tax on work as we get older, a tax that has become increasingly significant as benefits paid through the system have increased."

As for the earnings test for those over 65, it imposes an implicit marginal tax rate of over 75 percent on those who earn $10,000 a year, taking into account the payroll and income taxes on such earnings and adding them to the 50 percent reduction of Social Security benefits. Experience in Third World countries where such tax rates are regularly encountered has shown that people will not work when faced with such disincentives. The alternative prospect of leisure is too appealing. It is therefore a matter of economic common sense that the earnings test should be phased out, as Senator Barry Goldwater (R-Ariz.) has urged and as the administration plan enunciated by Secretary Schweiker has recommended. To be sure, ending the earnings test would add to the cost of Social Security, but this might in fact turn out to be much less than estimated: the additional income presently *not* being earned would be taxable.

Jim Storey [in *The Journal of the Institute for Socioeconomic Studies*] has aptly summarized these arguments as follows: "As the length of life is extended, and the years older people can spend in good health grow longer, it is simply not in the best interest of older workers to withdraw from the labor force. Unnecessary dependence on government transfer payments and employer pensions over long time periods under rapidly changing economic conditions is clearly unwise. And to consign . . . these potentially productive years to full retirement is not in the best interest of large numbers of older workers from the perspective of physical and mental well-being."

It is argued, of course, that people aged 62 and older are "entitled" to opt for early retirement. Incontestably, the law so reads. But Congress is similarly "entitled" to alter the system once again, just as it did in 1961. It is foolish to suggest that once the system has been changed in such a way as to encourage leisure it may no longer be changed again, at a time when it has become apparent that the subsidized leisure of early retirees is beyond the nation's economic capability.

This truth flies in the face of one of the most corruptive pieces of folk belief ever to enter the public consciousness— that "the United States is the richest nation in the world." The proposition is made, accordingly, that each and every cost can be borne. Because this false proposition is so widely accepted and deeply believed, its political implications are hard to resist. Nonetheless, responsible leaders, if such exist, must accept that at some point the increasingly onerous burden of Social Security taxes will alienate youthful workers forced to pay for the benefits enjoyed by slacking early retirees.

Indeed, the moment of truth may be no more distant than October 1982—if OMB Director Stockman's date proves right. Perhaps then, with Social Security reduced to the contours of the Kansas City Hyatt Regency, Congress will be encouraged to take another look at the way in which the Social Security system encourages people to stay home, to remain unproductive and off the payrolls.

THE SOLVENCY OF THE SOCIAL SECURITY SYSTEM[4]

The Short Term Financing Problem

The Social Security system is presently facing a short term financing problem in the OASI [Old Age and Survivors Insurance] program. Between 1982 and 1990, the reserve in the OASI trust fund will not be sufficient to cover an anticipated short fall in payroll tax revenues. This short term problem results from the higher than expected rates of inflation, unemployment and retirement which have occurred over the last several years and which have acted to reduce Social Security revenues and increase OASI benefit outlays. Using intermediate economic assumptions, the Social Security Trustees projected in their 1980 Report that OASI reserves would fall below the level required to avoid cash flow difficulties in 1982 and become exhausted in 1983. This situation will begin to correct itself in 1990 when OASI revenues once again exceed expenditures as a result of scheduled increases in Social Security payroll taxes and a projected decline in retirement rates. Subsequently, the fund will accumulate large reserves for several decades.

It is important to note that while there will be a short fall in the OASI program for the rest of the decade, the DI [Disability Insurance] and HI [Hospital Insurance] trust funds will have large reserves during this period. The reserve in the

[4] Excerpt from chapter entitled "The Structure and Solvency of Social Security," from *Keeping Social Security Strong—Analysis and Recommendations,* report of the New York State Task Force on Social Security. By permission of the New York State Office for the Aging.

DI trust, for example, is projected to reach 442 percent of annual expenditures by 1990. In fact, if the reserves of the three trust funds are added together, projections indicate that the reserves along with anticipated payroll tax revenues will be sufficient to cover the expenditures of all three programs throughout the entire decade. The Trustees projections indicate that combined OASI/DI/HI reserves would reach a low of 16 percent of annual expenditures in 1985 and would subsequently increase. Thus, even though there is a financing problem in one of its trust funds, the Social Security System as a whole is relatively sound.

In addition to the Social Security Trustees 1980 Report, it should be noted that other sources have provided projections on the short range financial solvency of the Social Security system and there has been some disagreement about the exact magnitude of the short term problem. For example, the Carter 1982 Budget Projections forecast a low in the combined reserves of 3 percent scheduled to occur in 1986. The Congressional Budget Office forecast a low of 7 percent in 1986. Under both of these forecasts, minor cash flow problems would occur in the system. The Reagan Administration has issued much different projections. Based upon what it terms to be "worst-case economic assumptions," the Administration has forecast a depleted combined reserve by 1985. It should be noted, however, that these worst-case projections were issued as supporting data for proposed cuts in Social Security benefits. Using assumptions based on "expected economic conditions," the Administration projects that the combined reserves never fall below 14 percent during the decade.

The Long Range Financing Problem

The long range financing problem facing Social Security also relates to the OASI program but will result from demographic trends rather than economic conditions. The Trustees project that the reserves of the OASI program will be depleted sometime after 2020 because of the changing ratio between workers and retirees that is expected to occur when the post war "baby boom" generation begins to retire in full force. Admitting that long range projections are extremely problematic, the Trustees have estimated this shortfall to be 1.5 percent of covered payroll or about 11 percent of program costs. The combined OASI and DI reserves are expected to be exhausted just after 2030. HI reserves are not included in these estimates because only 25 year forecasts are made for the HI program.

It appears that some long term change in the Social Security system will be necessary, but the exact magnitude of the change needed is difficult to determine at this time. Over a 75 year period, small changes in either economic or demographic assumptions can result in greatly varied projections of program costs. For example, according to "pessimistic" assumptions of the Trustees, the combined trust funds will be depleted soon after 2010, but according to the "optimistic" assumptions, the combined funds will end the 75 year projection period with substantial reserves. Understandably there is wide variation in opinion about the projected long range shortfall in the Social Security system. Former Social Security Commissioner Robert Ball contends that the Trustees' projections are based on too many assumptions that may prove inaccurate, and thus should not be used to justify reductions in Social Security benefits at this time.

The Medicare Financing Problem

Although the Hospital Insurance program which finances Medicare Part A Benefits currently has large reserves and will continue to accumulate reserves for several years, the program is expected to experience financing problems after this decade. In its 1980 Annual report, the Trustees projected that HI reserves will be depleted in 1994. Although the HI tax rate is already scheduled to increase in future years, hospital costs are projected to continue to grow more quickly than earnings and thus the currently enacted tax will eventually become inadequate. The HI trust is expected to remain depleted for the duration of the 25 year period for which the HI projections are made. The Medicare financing problem appears to be the most serious of the three problems facing the Social Security system.

THOSE FOULED-UP SOCIAL SECURITY CHECKS[5]

John Sabatini, the teenage son of a high Social Security official, was fired from his summer job at a Maryland fast-food restaurant for an unusual reason: He didn't have a Social Security number.

Sabatini had dutifully applied for a card at his local Social Security Administration office. The card just never arrived in time to please his boss.

That case, says congressional investigators and Social Security officials, is typical of a growing mountain of administrative foul-ups bedeviling the nation's 160-billion-dollar pension system.

Although less publicized than Social Security's severe financing problems, the blunders are wasting taxpayers' dollars and impairing service to the 155 million people on the system's rolls. For instance—

—In North Carolina, a retired bookkeeper was startled last summer when she received an adjustment in her monthly benefits check—an increase from $181.80 to $9,281.60. The proper increase should have been $20.80.

—A Bennington, Nebraska, widow became exasperated last fall after making several unsuccessful attempts—through the mail and by telephone—to halt a steady flow of monthly benefits checks addressed to her daughter. "They won't listen," she says. "I'm getting tired of it."

—Some beneficiaries have received benefits checks on which ZIP codes were substituted for dollar amounts.

—In case after case, recipients who change addresses get

[5] Reprint of magazine article by James M. Hildreth, associate editor. *U.S. News & World Report.* 92:67–8. F. 1, '82. Copyright 1982, U.S. News & World Report, Inc.

identical checks at both their new and old residences. Meanwhile, other recipients who move get no checks at all.

—In more than 8,000 cases, checks have been sent to people who have been dead for at least two years. Moreover, improper payments have been made to relatives of dead beneficiaries. Total cost to the system: An estimated 60 million dollars.

Poor service causes headaches, too. People frequently wait months to be issued Social Security cards, to receive reports on earnings histories or to receive determinations of their eligibility for Medicare. Some never get answers, officials say, unless they doggedly pursue matters.

All in all, acknowledges John Svahn, Social Security commissioner, "we have horrendous problems in providing services to taxpayers and beneficiaries."

A Joke

Many of today's woes can be traced directly back to the agency's antiquated, "patchwork" computer system. "Mere mention of the system is guaranteed to evoke gales of laughter and bouts of knee slapping among people in the computer-science field," says Jan Prokop, a former SSA associate commissioner.

One result of computer-system problems: A monumental backlog. Last June, for instance, the agency came within 18 hours of missing the mailing deadline for issuing Social Security checks with updated cost-of-living increases. Over a four-month period, employes spent 20,000 man-hours to program the computers plus 2,500 hours of computer time in order to make the changes. The same job could have been done in a relatively few days using a modern computer system, say officials.

At the same time, the agency maintains a mammoth file containing information on worker earnings, which the computers have been unable to match up with individuals' records. As a result, 69 billion dollars in earnings reported to SSA has not been credited to workers' accounts, says a government study. Some cases date back to 1937.

Just maintaining records of present workers and recipients is no small task. Every year, the agency is supposed to update information to reflect current earnings and benefits levels. The computers are still working on 1978 figures.

Over all, says Svahn, the system's processing is 15,000 hours in arrears and is falling behind at the rate of an additional 2,000 hours a month. "We're in a survival mode here," says Svahn. "Everybody hopes that 36 million benefits checks get out on time. As long as they do, we make it through another month."

It wasn't always this way. Twenty-five years ago, Social Security's IBM computer system was considered "state of the art"—the best available. But improvements to the system have been virtually nonexistent since that time.

Basic hardware is a major concern. Currently, the agency uses 15 mainframe computers located at a sprawling complex in a Baltimore suburb. Only 13 of the units are working. The other two have been cannibalized for spare parts because IBM doesn't manufacture the units used by the SSA any more.

Another huge problem is storage of computer records. The earnings and benefits histories for workers and recipients are maintained on what Svahn calls "archaic" magnetic tapes—500,000 of them. Just to move the daily supply of 14,000 reels to the computers takes an army of 2,000 employes.

Further complicating the process is the software system—programs that tell the computers what to do. "It's all ancient," grumbles Svahn. "We run some of our biggest operations on software that was developed for fancy adding machines back in the late 1950s."

Worse still, the system lacks blueprints for explaining how it works. This complicates the training of new workers. Last year, Social Security had to borrow a computer expert who had left the agency for another federal job. The reason: He was the only person who understood how the program worked.

Related to the computer difficulties is a morale problem

among workers at the Maryland complex. According to the General Accounting Office, Congress's watchdog agency, disgruntled employes committed 45 "malicious acts" of vandalism in computer areas during the four years that ended in February, 1981.

Fraud has surfaced as well. Two years ago, a benefits authorizer received a 10-year prison term after she was convicted of approving $500,000 worth of disability checks for nonexistent beneficiaries.

Major Upgrade

To correct some of the ills, Svahn says he will soon unveil a five-year blueprint to modernize the entire system. The plan will involve updating the computers, strengthening management and improving services to the public. The estimated cost: Up to 600 million dollars.

"My goal is not to fix it tomorrow, because I can't do that," says Svahn. But if his plan is adopted by higher-ups in the government, and Congress provides the money, the system can be improved enough to "provide services that people are entitled to."

One aim: Install direct computer links with Social Security's 1,344 field offices to allow individuals to get instant answers to questions about their benefits entitlements—much as airline-reservations systems supply quick facts on flights.

Will Congress go along with these major improvements? Probably. Many lawmakers are aware of the troubles, thanks to 32 separate GAO reports since 1974. "We're ready to move," says an aide to Representative J. J. Pickle (D-Tex.), chairman of the House Social Security Subcommittee.

Meanwhile, citizen complaints and demands for service continue to grow—taxing the system's facilities and personnel. Relates Svahn: "During the weekend of January 9–10, I talked at home with an 87-year-old lady from California who was very upset about a problem she was having with benefits. She called me 23 times."

THE CASHING OF SOCIAL SECURITY CHECKS FOR DEAD RELATIVES[6]

Many an American was shocked last fall to the point of anger when the federal government disclosed that upwards of $60 million was paid in Social Security benefits to 8,518 people listed on Medicare records as dead.

It was obvious that the U.S. government, with all its might and investigatory apparatus, was lax in allowing such a blunder—one stretching back 15 years. Once again, we have a glaring example of the unfortunate truth that many people regard Uncle Sam as a distant, rich relative unworthy of respect and deserving to be defrauded at the first opportunity.

Here are some cases uncovered by the Inspector General's office of the Department of Health and Human Services.

—A retired vice president of a substantial corporation appeared to be the model of respectability in his mansion in a Midwest city. He and his wife deposited their Social Security checks in a joint account, but he failed to notify the government when she died, continued depositing her checks and used the proceeds himself.

—A Baltimore man, John Sydnor Jr., apparently shot himself in the head in a public park in mid-September after agreeing to a second meeting with an FBI agent to discuss his dead father's checking account. According to a government investigator, Sydnor's father died in May 1977, and John Sydnor Jr. siphoned $14,250 from his father's checking account, some of the funds apparently representing Social Security checks deposited after his death. So now father and son are dead.

—A widow in a Gulf Coast seaport was pleased that her husband's Social Security checks kept coming after he died. According to government investigators, she evidently forged

---

[6] Reprint of magazine article by Nick Thimmesch, columnist. *Saturday Evening Post.* p 38+. Ja./F. '82. By permission of the author.

his signature and cashed the checks. Confronted by an agent, she claimed her husband was still alive but at sea on a shrimp boat and unavailable. The agent checked local records and learned that the man was indeed dead. The widow confessed.

—A Roman Catholic nun died, and for two years, her Social Security checks continued to be received at the convent where she lived and deposited in the convent's account. The ecclesiastical authorities were unable to give the government agent a satisfactory explanation for the failure to report the nun's death to the Social Security Administration.

—A middle-aged businessman, regarded as wealthy, lived in his deceased father's large home and cashed his father's Social Security checks for many months after he died. The businessman explained to investigators that he needed the money to maintain adequate cash-flow in his business.

—A candidate for the state senate in an industrial state was discovered to have cashed his dead aunt's Social Security checks. The fact that he used this money for campaign expenses made the Inspector General's Office regard his case as "rather aggravated."

—A twin brother failed to report his twin's death and decided to cash his Social Security checks by posing as his brother when presenting those checks for payment. The surviving twin went to a different banking institution to cash his own Social Security checks.

—A woman whose sister had died cashed the deceased's Social Security checks. After the Inspector General's Office learned of the death through Medicare records, the woman was questioned. She first claimed her sister was alive but on a trip to Europe. Confronted with the records, she tearfully confessed.

In these cases, the evidence makes the parties involved appear culpable on the question of intent. But there are hundreds of other cases where people received a dead person's Social Security checks and just squirreled them away. In Southwest Texas, investigators recovered 125 uncashed Social Security checks totaling $63,000. They had been sent to someone who died in 1967 and kept by a relative. As of November 1981, the government had not filed charges against the person who kept the checks.

Such cases, whether they represent intentional fraud or irresponsibility and laziness by a citizen, have created quite a stir in the bureaucracy, especially since the Reagan administration has vowed to cut costs and make the government more efficient.

"It's absolutely amazing that it's been allowed to exist," said John A. Svahn, appointed as Social Security Commissioner by President Ronald Reagan. "But I'm not embarrassed by it. I'm trying to find out all instances where something like this does exist so we can stop it."

The Social Security Administration, which sent out about $150 billion in 1981 to 36 million recipients of its three principal benefits programs, until recently simply had no idea who among the 28 million recipients of retirement benefits (about $99 billion) was alive and who might be dead.

"Social Security operates on the notion that its basic responsibility is to deliver services to the recipients," said Richard P. Kusserow, Inspector General of the Department of Health and Human Services. "The benefit of the doubt usually goes to the recipient. If a person says, 'I didn't get my check this month,' a new check is issued. We don't wait until there is an investigation. The idea at Social Security is that somebody 65 or older is really dependent on that money, is entitled to it and should get it."

Just to contemplate the human and machine activity involved in preparing, mailing and accounting in one year for nearly 432 million individual checks is to begin to comprehend the enormity of the Social Security system.

Since the Social Security Administration had its hands full just getting the mountain of monthly checks out, it evidently had no time or inclination to diligently and systematically keep track of who was alive and who was dead among its recipients.

According to Kusserow, another Reagan appointee, the Social Security Administration relied on notification by funeral homes, who collected lump-sum benefit checks, or someone close to the deceased in order to strike names from the rolls of those receiving benefit checks.

Then, in the summer of 1981, Kusserow approved a spot check on recipient records to determine whether checks were being sent to dead people. This was accomplished by pulling the names of Medicare recipients who had died from the records and matching them—by computer—with master reels of people still receiving retirement benefit checks.

"Since 90 percent of the people on Medicare are also getting retirement checks," explained Kusserow, "we had a good way to compare. When a person on Medicare dies, his physician sends us that one last bill for payment and states that his patient has died.

"Even then we're not sure, because a person making that identification, even a physician, sometimes doesn't put down the deceased's Social Security number or puts down a wrong number. Government forms are not perfect.

"So out of humanitarian consideration, Social Security is very careful about quickly knocking somebody's name off the rolls. Older people need that money. They get cut off, and they starve. So the Social Security people want hard information."

After 8,518 names of dead people still getting checks turned up, and with the prospect that more such "cross-checking" might increase the number to 10,000 and beyond, Kusserow decided on his own to make this project a permanent operation of his department.

His office has already found that 1,200 recipients of Black Lung Disease benefits are also dead. So now he's running cross-checks of other beneficiary lists—those on Disability Insurance, for example. The General Accounting Office, by the way, estimated in early 1981 that 20 percent of the 2.8 million disability beneficiaries are actually able to work.

"The assumption by Social Security that running this investigation wasn't worth doing was wrong," Kusserow said. "It is up to us to see that it doesn't happen again. If the system isn't working it must be corrected. Social Security has to live with the consequences or report to congressional oversight. Three committees charged with this are the House Subcommittee on Social Security, the Senate Subcommittee on Social Security and the House Subcommittee on Intergovernmental Relations and Human Resources.

"Let's face it, our goal is to reduce overhead and deliver services. If the system is wasteful, full of fraud and abuse, then less money comes out at the recipients' end. But it works both ways; if you do investigations, you might find cases of people not getting what they deserve. It's my job to stop the hemorrhaging."

Still, despite these statements worthy of praise, the government's record of surveillance, investigation and prosecution involving the Social Security system is only fair at best. Few traces are run on cases where individuals claim they didn't receive checks. Of the $60 million in checks sent to dead people, only $2 million had been recovered five months after the investigation began. And of the 8,518 cases investigated, fewer than 100 were being prosecuted at the end of 1981, though hundreds of others were being considered for presentation to federal courts.

"Charges can be filed by the U.S. Attorney only if he can prove intent," Kusserow explained. "It's not always easy to prove intent. A spouse might not know she wasn't supposed to keep or cash a check. How do you prosecute an 86-year-old geriatric? But if the party in question is a younger relative, or a nonrelative, or a payee-agency such as a nursing home, then there seems to be little excuse.

"It must also be remembered that the justice system doesn't move that fast. It will take a while to track down all these cases. We're also working on Social Security employees who might be involved."

In the years before the current investigation was begun, there was a scattering of cases involving Social Security employees who, on learning of a recipient's death, changed the name of the payee on the rolls to another name and had the checks routed to himself or herself. The Social Security system allows the name of a second party—the payee—to receive checks for a recipient and cash them.

Kusserow's office is investigating the possibility of "insiders" defrauding the government in this episode involving the dead recipients. "Insiders" are far easier to prosecute than, say, the little old lady who received her dead husband's checks and put them away in the bureau drawer.

Or how about the case of the Hollywood comedian, known to everyone in the country, who died several years back and continued to receive his Social Security checks. Government investigators learned that his agent had 39 of these checks. Again the question of intent. What was the dead comic's agent going to do with them?

And how about the case of the mother-in-law who lived with her son and her daughter-in-law in the latter's house? When the couple divorced, the mother-in-law remained in the house with her daughter-in-law. The mother-in-law eventually died, and her Social Security checks continued coming to the daughter-in-law.

By the time the government got involved, the daughter-in-law was explaining that she had put the checks on a fence-post every month for the mailman to pick up. So investigators checked the mailman, the post-office inspector and back with the daughter-in-law. Her story, according to Kusserow's office, remains unverified, and she is under suspicion. No charges have been filed—yet.

Another case involves a woman whose father died in 1968. Not only did she keep Social Security checks for him amounting to $38,000, but she told government investigators that she also was holding $25,500 in pension checks sent that dead man by his long-time employer. The government confiscated both batches of checks.

Kusserow shakes his head over cases like these. He'd like to see wrongdoers punished (up to five years and/or $10,000 fines in most cases), but he is aware that hoarding and squirreling away are instincts many people give in to.

He is well trained for the post to which Reagan named him last spring. Kusserow had been a special agent in the FBI for 13 years, specializing in white-collar crime. He was prominent in FBI investigations of bank fraud in the Chicago area and had also done considerable work with investigations of labor and government racketeering.

"I am a presidential appointee and report to the Congress and to the Secretary of Health and Human Services," he said, by way of stating the independence of his office. "I don't ask permission from anybody for what I do here.

"But I am aware that this administration is very much concerned about cutting down fraud and abuse and making the system work. Sixty million dollars may seem like a drop in the bucket in a system pumping out $150 billion a year, but that $60 million can sure be used by the Commissioner [Svahn] when he's faced with cutting back payments."

III. THE REFORM DEBATE

EDITOR'S INTRODUCTION

There are a variety of proposed reforms by individuals and by the federal government which were projected in the hope that the Social Security system can be solvent again and be free of abuses.

Raising the retirement age is the most popular and the most controversial proposal. A Social Security task force appointed by Jimmy Carter suggested such a reform measure. In the first selection, from the *U.S. News & World Report*, Rita Ricardo-Campbell of the Hoover Institution of Stanford University, and Betty Duskin, Director of Research, the National Council of Senior Citizens, debate the merits of raising the eligibility age. Ms. Ricardo-Campbell contends that medical advances, demographics, the natural reluctance to retire, and economic common sense all point to raising the retirement age. Ms. Duskin disagrees, arguing that health advances are not as promising and life-saving as Ms. Ricardo-Campbell claims.

The next two authors support Ms. Ricardo-Campbell's view. A. F. Ehrbar justifies this argument in *Fortune* by citing two studies: the Michael J. Boskin Study, which calculates that moving the retirement age to 68 will preserve the system, and the Robert Myer study, which reveals that a man of 68.9 years will have the same life expectancy as a 65-year-old had when the Social Security system was introduced. Ehrbar also proposes additional reforms that would base cost of living increases in benefits on prices, rather than on wage increases, thus adjusting increases more to inflation. He also calls for taxing Social Security benefits and elimination of payments to 18- to 21-year-old survivors and minimum benefits to those who do not qualify for Social Security. Not only does sociologist Eli Ginzberg feel that the retirement age should be raised and that Social Security benefits should be taxed, but he also proposes in *Scientific American*, that reforms be built into the system to correct inequities for women and those poor elderly who are below the poverty line. All for taxing Social Security benefits, Dr. Leonard M. Greene, president of the Institute for Socioeconomic Studies, also urges in the fourth article the elimination of the retirement earnings test, whereby Social Security benefit deductions are pegged to earnings.

The Reagan administration introduced its own Social Security reform plan on May 12, 1981. In contrast to proposals already outlined, President Reagan's prescription to cure the "sick" Social Security system included reducing benefits for new retirees, setting maximum family benefits for new enrollees, tightening eligibility requirements for disability payments, and curbing "double dipping," where ex-federal workers get both pensions and Social Security payments of $122 per month. The fifth and sixth articles, from *Time* and *U.S. News & World Report*, analyze the President's plan. They also survey the congressional reaction which culminated in a "sense of the Senate resolution" condemning the plan by an astounding vote of 96 to 0.

Newsweek analyzes the President's defeat in the seventh selection and sets the stage in Congress for the next of many rounds in a politically hazardous battle in which the main protagonists are clearly drawn. Then, in this connection, George Church of *Time* Magazine, ties his reform proposals in with the political debate they can be expected to generate. He discusses specific short-term reforms for the immediate "cash crisis" and long-term reforms to avoid the "long-range demographic disaster," but he is not optimistic about Congressional concurrence on any of them.

Three speeches showing congressional reaction are reprinted from *Congressional Quarterly* and conclude this section. The first was made by the chairman of the Sub-Committee on Social Security of the House Committee on Ways and Means, Democratic Representative J. J. (Jake) Pickle, who is seeking a compromise between all contending factions. In his oral summary of his bill in the House of Representatives, he includes a number of reforms called for in earlier articles in this section. The second speech, by Republican Senator Robert Dole, pretty much ignores other proposals and calls for more lasting reforms, instead of temporary measures to stave off bankruptcy now. Finally, Democratic Senator Joseph Biden spares no criticism for Administration cuts, taking the position that it would put many elderly people below the poverty line. The trustee report and the summer debate over President Reagan's plan prodded Congress to begin earnest consideration of a number of reform packages. But throughout the fall of 1981, both houses failed to reach a consensus in devising a reform program. Facing elections in November 1982, foot-dragging will, no doubt be evident in Congress and it appears that Social Security reform will become ever more pressing and slow to come.

PRO AND CON: RAISE SOCIAL SECURITY RETIREMENT AGE[1]

Interview with Rita Ricardo-Campbell, Senior Fellow,
Hoover Institution, Stanford University

Yes—"The financial structure of the system will be strengthened."

Q. *Mrs. Campbell, why do you favor raising the eligibility age for receiving full Social Security benefits?*

A. There are two main reasons: The first is a changed demographic picture since the Social Security Act was originally passed by Congress in 1935; the other is increased life expectancy.

With the exception of the baby boom of the post-World War II period, we've had a declining birth rate. But the baby

---

[1] Reprint of interview entitled "Pro and Con: Raise the Retirement Age," *U.S. News & World Report.* 91:35. Jl. 27, '81. Copyright 1981, U.S. News & World Report, Inc.

boom produced 75 million Americans who are now between 17 and 35 years old. These people will reach retirement age in the next century. Then there will be 2 workers for each Social Security beneficiary, compared with 5 workers for each beneficiary in 1960. By the year 2050, the aged will constitute 19 percent of the population, compared with 11 percent now. By gradually raising the retirement age, the financial structure of the system will be strengthened. For instance, you would save half of 1 percent of payroll for each year that retirement is postponed.

Q. *What about life expectancy?*
A. Since Social Security began, life expectancy has increased dramatically. At birth, men can now expect to live, on average, three years longer and women six years longer. If a man retires at age 67, he still has more than 10 years ahead of him to enjoy life.

Q. *Opponents of a higher retirement age acknowledge that life expectancy has increased but say that health problems of the elderly play a major role in retirement decisions. Do you agree?*
A. If you ask people after they're in retirement why they retired, it sounds great to say you weren't feeling so well. But if you ask people prospectively, it is quite clear that health is not the major reason; it is whether, in their opinion, they will have enough money to live on.

Q. *How fast should the retirement age be increased?*
A. Very gradually. There is nothing we can do immediately about mandating or postponing retirement ages. People should have warning so they can plan their retirement and also to minimize the inequities. Another reason for gradualism is that company pension plans are integrated with Social Security. They will have to be adjusted.

Q. *Can people remain truly productive past age 65?*
A. I think a worker's experience counts for something. In-

tellectual vigor doesn't necessarily decrease at age 65. People can continue to put out very good work. Your thinking is not cut off at that age. The average older worker is needed in today's labor force to keep up productivity because of the young people and inexperienced women who are entering the labor force in greater numbers than ever before.

Interview with Betty Duskin, Director of Research, National Council of Senior Citizens

No—"It is a reduction in benefits based on bad assumptions."

Q. *Ms. Duskin, why do you oppose raising the age for receiving full Social Security benefits to above 65?*
A. Because it is a reduction in benefits based on bad assumptions. Proponents of changing the age to 67 or 68 assume that because life expectancy has increased in this century, health expectancy has improved in an equivalent way. Evidence doesn't support that.

Q. *What do you mean?*
A. Certainly, health has improved, but primarily because of a reduction in illnesses of infancy and early childhood. But we haven't conquered arthritis and emphysema. Most of the gains in life expectancy occur during early years, not the middle or later years of life. This argues against an increased ability to work longer.

Q. *So you want to preserve people's freedom to retire as their personal circumstances require.*
A. Yes. I think that it is necessary. Different people have different reasons for retiring when they do—and most of those reasons don't involve a voluntary choice.

Q. *Is there any magic in the age of 65?*
A. It's an acquired magic. It's something we're used to. It is also something private pension systems are quite used to. Any change in the Social Security retirement age is going to stand private industry on its head.

Q. *Federal law bars companies from forcing retirements before 70. Does this contradict the eligibility age for Social Security?*

A. Not really. It's appropriate to make social policy that will encourage people who can work longer to do so. However, doing it with a stick instead of a carrot is not only punitive but futile. For example, what about someone with a severe case of hypertension who is forced to remain in a stressful job because he can't afford to retire? The lack of choice may kill him. But his survivors will live on to collect benefits. Nothing is saved, but a lot of harm will have been done.

Q. *What about those people who decide on early retirement but are in relatively good health?*

A. Only a small percentage do so. The majority retire before age 65 because of ill health or because they are eased out or pushed out of a job. And so they reluctantly take the option of early retirement. It's not a voluntary choice.

Q. *The latest Social Security trustees' report says it will take 2 workers to support each retiree in the 21st century. Doesn't something drastic have to be done to avert dire problems?*

A. Those problems don't exist with certainty, and changing the rules in Social Security wouldn't solve such problems anyway. We should really address ourselves to increasing productivity—and to a potential labor shortage in the next century.

HOW TO SAVE SOCIAL SECURITY[2]

. . . Two simple changes would eliminate the need for any payroll tax increases beyond the level now set for 1990. One is

[2] Excerpt from magazine article by A. F. Ehrbar, staff writer. *Fortune.* 102:37–8. Ag. 25, '80. Excerpted from the August 25 issue of FORTUNE Magazine by special permission. Copyright 1980 Time Inc.

to raise the retirement age, starting in the year 2000, from 65 to 68. A new study by four economists at the National Bureau of Economic Research shows that such a change would eliminate the long-term deficit in the Old Age and Survivors portion of Social Security. Using the Social Security Administration's intermediate projection, the economists calculated that the present value of the old-age deficit is about $885 billion. That is, the old-age benefits that will be paid over the next 75 years—discounted to the present at a 3 percent real interest rate—are $885 billion more than the old-age portion of the payroll taxes that will be collected.

The total deficit, including the hospital portion of Medicare and disability benefits, is much larger. Stanford economist Michael J. Boskin, who headed the National Bureau study team, figures that the hospital and disability deficits come to 50 percent to 70 percent of the old-age deficit. That puts the present value of the total Social Security deficit at $1.3 trillion to $1.5 trillion—more than double the national debt.

When Boskin's team calculated the effect of raising the retirement age to 68, they came up with a $200-billion surplus in the old-age portion of the system. Says Boskin, a 34-year-old baby-boomer who advocates later retirement: "Altering the length of retirement by a single year, by changing either the retirement age or life expectancy, raises or lowers the Social Security deficit by about $350 billion."

A Case for Later Retirement

While raising the retirement age obviously amounts to a benefit cut, it wouldn't mean a large reduction in the length of retirement. Robert Myers, a former chief actuary of Social Security and another proponent of later retirement, estimates that a man 68.9 years old in the year 2000 will have the same life expectancy a 65-year-old had when the Social Security Act was passed in 1935; for women, life expectancy at 72.5 will be the same as it was at age 65 in 1935.

Boskin and Myers have a lot of support in their call for a later retirement age. The National Commission on Social Security, set up by Congress to evaluate possible changes in the system, has tentatively endorsed a plan to raise the eligibility age to 68 over a 12-year period starting in 2000. The President's Commission has recommended that Congress consider raising the age, and the last two Social Security Advisory Councils have supported the idea. The councils are groups that assess the state of the system every four years.

Most of the opposition to later retirement comes from Social Security expansionists like former Commissioner Robert Ball, old-age lobbyists like the American Association of Retired Persons, and Congressmen. In 1977, Barber Conable, the ranking Republican on the Ways and Means Committee, proposed a plan similar to the one endorsed by the National Commission. Conable couldn't even muster the support of the Republicans on the committee, but he did draw 3,000 letters from enraged Gray Panthers.

Price Indexing vs. Wage Indexing

The other change that would bring large savings is an adjustment in the benefit formula that Congress adopted in 1977. That formula ties initial benefit levels to average wages. That is, future retirees will be entitled to benefits that rise by the same amount as average wages until a person is 60; after that, an individual's benefits are tied to the C.P.I. Since wages rise faster than prices over the long run, benefits paid to future retirees will be higher than the present ones, even in constant dollars. The idea behind the formula, called "wage indexing," is to assure that pensions replace a constant percentage of pre-retirement income.

An alternative is to index initial benefits to prices instead of wages. Under that formula Social Security would gradually replace a smaller percentage of pre-retirement income, but it would provide future retirees with at least as much purchasing power as persons retiring this year. In fact, the formula

for determining initial benefits would cause them to continue
to rise in real terms, though at a slower rate. In 1977, a congressional consulting panel headed by Harvard economist
William C. Hsaio estimated that a worker with average earnings who retires in 2050 would get a pension with a real value
of triple the current benefit under wage indexing and double
the present benefit under price indexing. Hsaio, who favors
price indexing, figures it would save roughly the same amount
as raising the retirement age.

In addition to reducing costs, price indexing would boost
private savings and economic growth. Social Security cuts
into savings by diminishing the need to provide for retirement—though the magnitude of the effect is a matter of hot
dispute. Studies by Martin Feldstein, president of the National Bureau of Economic Research and another price-in-
dexing proponent, indicate that Social Security may reduce
private savings by as much as 38 percent.

If we changed the benefit formula and raised the retirement age, the combined cost savings would wipe out the entire long-term Social Security deficit and leave room for a
payroll tax cut sometime after the year 2000. The lower costs
would also give Congress the flexibility it will need to correct
some of the system's deficiencies, such as the inequitable
treatment of working wives.

Billion-Dollar Nibbles

Under current law a couple gets 150 percent of the husband's basic pension while both are alive, and the survivor
gets 100 percent after one of the two dies. That benefit
usually is greater than what working wives can collect on
their own earnings (they can't take both), so most of them get
nothing in return for the payroll taxes they pay. Since Congress isn't likely to repeal the 50 percent bonus for housewives, correcting the mistreatment of working wives will be
expensive. And with a majority of wives now in the labor
force, voters are bound to demand some such change.

Unfortunately, Congress has no similarly simple options for dealing with Social Security's short-term financial troubles. Slashing benefits to current retirees still is politically unthinkable; it also would be morally indefensible to cut payments to persons who depend on Social Security just to get by. However, a handful of unnecessary benefits could be eliminated without harming the truly needy. The cuts would be puny relative to total costs, but just nibbling at Social Security can save several billion dollars a year.

One potential cut is the payment to survivors between 18 and 21 years old who are full-time students. The benefit was added in 1965, before Congress created the panoply of college-assistance programs available now. Another benefit that could go is the payment to surviving spouses with 16- and 17-year-old children. The reasoning behind the benefit is that single parents aren't able to work, but that obviously isn't the case when children reach 16. A third prospective cut is the $255 lump-sum death benefit, originally meant to cover burial costs.

The benefit most deserving of elimination is the so-called minimum payment, intended to help persons whose covered earnings were too low to qualify for even a subsistence-level pension. The prime beneficiaries now are federal employees. Though exempt from Social Security taxes, many moonlight in order to qualify for the minimum pension. The Congressional Budget Office estimates that those four cuts, all of which were proposed by President Carter last year, would save $3.2 billion a year by fiscal 1985.

Penalizing the Industrious

Two other desirable reforms would actually entail higher costs, but would make the system fairer. One is to get rid of the earnings test for retirees between 65 and 72. They now lose 50 cents in benefits for every dollar they earn over $5,-000. The provision, which exacts a large penalty from poor retirees who want to supplement their benefits, doesn't affect those with substantial capital income or private pensions. In effect, the system applies a means test to beneficiaries who work but not to those who are idle.

Eliminating the earnings test for people 65 and over would be surprisingly cheap. Last year the Social Security Administration saved only $2.1 billion by reducing the benefits of workers who earned too much. The full cost wouldn't even be that high because many retirees would work more— and so pay more Social Security and income taxes—if they didn't have to sacrifice benefits.

The second reform, and the most controversial of all possible changes, is to reverse the income-tax treatment of Social Security—tax the benefits and exempt the payroll taxes. The common view, of course, is that benefits should be tax-exempt because retirees paid for them with after-tax dollars. In fact, Social Security is a welfare system that dispenses benefits on the basis of past earnings instead of need, with proportionately larger payments going to low earners. The Internal Revenue Service (not Congress) originally exempted the benefits from income taxes in 1940 precisely because they were welfare payments. Moreover, the taxes a worker pays have no direct relation to the benefits he receives; taxes are determined by the cost of paying benefits to others during the years he works.

The case for taxing Social Security benefits rests on the enormous wealth transfers the system effects—not just from high earners to low earners, but also from one age group to another. . . . [Boskin and his associates] defined a transfer as the difference between the pension benefits a person will receive and what he could have earned by investing the old-age portion of his taxes (including the part paid by the employer) in an annuity with a 3 percent real return. They found that persons born before 1913 who survived to collect benefits will, on average, receive net transfers of nearly $60,000 in 1980 dollars. In other words, persons born before 1913 "paid for" only 14 percent of the benefits they will collect. The other 86 percent is a windfall. In contrast, persons born between 1943 and 1952 will pay $374 more in taxes than they'll collect in retirement benefits, and persons born after 1952 will suffer successively larger losses.

A Subsidy for High Earners

Some wealth transfer from the richer working-age generation to the poorer retired generation is justifiable. But Social Security makes glaringly inequitable transfers from poor young workers to rich retirees. As Boskin says, "It makes little sense for current unskilled workers to surrender income to subsidize retired doctors and lawyers beyond fair returns on the taxes they paid."

Reversing the tax treatment would help redress that imbalance. Exempting young workers from income taxes on their "contributions" would reduce their total Social Security losses somewhat because the value of the tax savings would be greater than the taxes they would eventually pay on benefits. The deduction would be worth more to high-income individuals in higher tax brackets, but they ultimately would pay higher taxes on benefits; on balance, over their lifetimes, the change probably wouldn't have much effect on the wealth transfers among workers the same age.

The change would be fair to retirees as long as they were taxed only on benefits over and above the payroll taxes they paid into the system—a tax treatment identical with that now given to employee thrift plans, where workers invest after-tax dollars and pay taxes only on the earnings. Including benefits in taxable income wouldn't penalize the elderly poor; some 60 percent of Social Security recipients would pay no taxes at all.

A case can be made that an elderly couple with $15,000 of income from Social Security and a private pension deserves preferential tax treatment. But a stronger case can be made for a worker with a wife and two or three children and the same income. His Social Security payroll deduction this year will be $919.50, on which he'll pay another $130 or more of income taxes.

In 1978, the change would have cost $5.4 billion in lost

income-tax revenues. Mickey D. Levy of the American Enterprise Institute made a study of the effects of various tax treatments of Social Security and found that exempting payroll taxes would have reduced income-tax revenues by $9.4 billion in 1978. Including benefits (in excess of payroll taxes paid) in the recipients' taxable income would have increased revenues by $4 billion, and taxing all benefits would have boosted revenues $6.9 billion.

A Passion for Camouflaging Costs

The political history of Social Security gives little reason for optimism about any of these reforms, with the possible exception of eliminating the earnings test. Congress has frequently boosted benefits over the years, comfortable in the knowledge that the full bill for its vote-getting largess would come due only in the distant future. In the process, Social Security has evolved from a reasonably modest program to keep the elderly out of extreme poverty into a full-blown federal pension system.

Congressmen frequently talk of reforming the system, especially now that some of the formerly distant costs are driving up the tax rate. But the talk focuses more on camouflaging costs than on reducing them. Says Jake Pickle, chairman of the Ways and Means subcommittee on Social Security: "We've had 120 bills to freeze the taxes, but nobody's talking about cutting those benefits. If somebody does say he's going to cut benefits, we may want to freeze him."

The forces working against change are formidable. Cutting current benefits would anger the elderly, more of whom vote than any other age group, yet it wouldn't save enough to permit a sizable tax cut. Cutting future benefits is politically expensive because the elderly, ever watchful, see any reduction as a precedent that threatens their own benefits.

"This Craven Collective"

Barber Conable, weary and bent from previous battles, is despondent about the prospects for heading off the long-term crisis. "We should be able to design a system based on the facts of the baby boom," he says. "But it's going to take a Congress that is politically accountable, and this Congress is not. This craven collective will break and run as soon as they get 300 letters on a subject."

Still, under pressure from a public indignant over big increases in an extremely visible tax, Congress and the White House may be starting to move away from the traditional politics of Social Security. President Carter's proposal to cut certain benefits last year was a remarkable event. Though Congress rejected the cuts out of hand, a few Democrats on Ways and Means are starting to talk as though some reductions might really be possible at last. Pickle, for one, has been saying that a later retirement age might be possible. And Jim Jones of Oklahoma, an influential young member of the committee, hopes to engineer a major overhaul of the system next year.

Jones believes that public outrage over . . . January's payroll tax increase, combined with the looming 1984 deficiency in the trust funds and the bad news about the long-term deficit that will be coming out in the final reports of the National Commission and the President's Commission, will force Congress to act. "The average Congressman has put Social Security out of his mind," Jones says. "But the events of history are converging, and the public will demand that we do something." Jones's assessment that the nation at last has an opportunity to get control of the largest "uncontrollable" in the budget seems correct, but the opportunity is sure to dwindle if Congress delays for long.

THE SOCIAL SECURITY SYSTEM[3]

The real challenge to Social Security lies in the future. The proportion of the U.S. population 65 years old and older

[3] Article by Eli Ginzburg, sociologist. *Scientific American.* 246:55–7. Ja. '82. Reprinted with permission.

has been growing (from 9.2 percent in 1960 to 11.2 percent last year) and will continue to grow (to an estimated 12.2 percent in the year 2000). Retired people and their spouses are living longer: in 1950 the average life expectancy at 65 was another 13 years for men and 15 years for women, whereas in 1980 it reached 15 years for men and 20 years for women. The key factor in determining the financial integrity of the Social Security system is the relation between the number of workers paying taxes and the number of retired workers, dependents and survivors entitled to benefits. In 1945 there were 50 workers paying taxes to support current payments to each beneficiary; now each beneficiary is supported by about three workers, and in 2035 the ratio may be less than two taxpayers per beneficiary.

The long-term outlook has been appraised by the secretaries of Health and Human Services, Labor and the Treasury, who serve as the trustees of the Social Security system. In their 1980 report they estimated the average annual balance of revenue and expenditures for the next 75 years, assuming that there will be no change in the currently prescribed tax-base and tax-rate increases. The estimates were made under three sets of assumptions: optimistic, intermediate and pessimistic. Between 1980 and 2004, the trustees reported, the system as a whole should have an annual surplus of revenue over expenditures. In the next 25-year period the intermediate projection puts the annual deficit at about $12 billion. Between 2030 and 2054 the intermediate projection puts the deficit at about $46 billion per year.

The most obvious cure for a deficit is an increase in taxes. Last March the National Commission on Social Security estimated the increase in tax revenues that would be needed to keep the system in balance, assuming that some modest benefit changes recommended by the commission are enacted by Congress. The total tax (the employee's share plus the employer's) is already scheduled to rise from 13.4 percent this year to 15.3 percent in 1990. Additional increases would be necessary, raising the total to 15.7 percent between 2005 and

2009, to 20 percent between 2020 and 2024 and to 23.8 percent between 2035 and 2039. The commission saw two dangers in allowing the payroll tax to rise to these levels: the tax bite might be too big for young workers and other workers earning low wages, and the employers' share of the tax might discourage hiring. The commission therefore recommended that the payroll tax be limited to 18 percent, with the difference between that amount and the recommended tax level being covered from general revenues.

Is a rise of nearly 80 percent in the Social Security tax burden out of the question? Clearly the commission did not think so. The social security systems in some countries of Western Europe have a payroll-tax rate (employee plus employer) of between 18 and 28 percent. In return for higher taxes they supply more comprehensive benefits. Contributions for other public and private social programs can push the total levy in those countries up to 50 percent of a worker's earnings.

Before considering further the financing of the Social Security system, it should be asked whether the benefits now provided by the system are adequate. I would submit that there is room for improvement in the system, and the improvements would add to future costs. Among the conspicuous problems are the inadequacy of the present minimum benefit, inequities for women and the ineffective response of Medicare to the health-care needs of the elderly.

Every retired worker eligible for any benefits receives at least $122 per month. Those who get this minimum benefit are mainly women who worked for very low wages. In 1979 the Advisory Council on Social Security Financing and Benefits held that "single people who have worked full time at the federal minimum wage do not now receive a benefit sufficient to keep them out of poverty." The Advisory council recommended corrective action. President Reagan went in the opposite direction: he recommended eliminating the minimum benefit on the ground that it is a windfall for people who have retired on other federal pensions but who also barely qualify for Social Security. Congress went along with the President in the first round of budget cutting but restored the minimum payment last fall. It remains inadequate.

When the Social Security system was established, it dealt with women primarily as dependents or survivors. That has changed with the entry of large numbers of women into the work force. By 1978 two in every five female beneficiaries were receiving benefits by reason of their own work, not as a consequence of their marriage; the proportion is likely to increase to 80 percent for women who reach 65 in 2000. Women workers pay the same payroll tax as men, but many women receive higher benefits as dependents than as retired workers because the replacement rate is skewed to their disadvantage. One perverse result is that a 65-year-old couple get 17 percent more in benefits if only one of them was a wage earner than they do if both earned equal amounts. If a woman is divorced before the 10th year of a marraige, she receives no benefits when her former husband retires; if the marriage lasts for 10 years, she receives the full spouse's benefit.

One proposal that might lead to fairer treatment of women is an earnings-sharing plan. Benefits would be based on the combined earnings of the couple, whether or not both had worked and regardless of how much each had earned and therefore paid in Social Security taxes. In effect all earnings would be vested equally in the husband and the wife. The Advisory Council favors moving toward such a plan but suggests that more study is needed to be sure dependent's and survivor's benefits now accruing to many women are not jeopardized. For now the council has recommended two steps. It would allow a surviving spouse to have benefits based on the couple's combined earnings, and it would adopt a limited form of earnings sharing for divorced couples.

Medicare now covers only about 40 percent of the medical costs of the elderly. It largely covers acute hospital care and, for those who elect to buy supplementary medical insurance, physicians' services. Each year a considerable number of older people have very large medical expenses (more than $2,500 or $3,000) that they must pay from their own funds.

Much of the care required for chronic conditions is simply not covered. Medicare makes no contribution toward helping a patient remain in his own home with home nursing or attendants when he is chronically sick or feeble, and it makes no significant contribution toward paying the cost of his staying in a nursing home. In failing to support care in the patient's home or in a nursing home Medicare encourages unnecessary hospital stays and thus runs up the country's total health-care bill. In spite of these serious shortcomings, the hospital-insurance tax rate will increase sharply beginning in the 1990s.

The demographic imperatives and the need for improvements in Social Security benefits provoke a series of questions. The first is: Can payroll-tax increases sustain the system into the middle of the next century? A moderate increase in the tax rate is certainly feasible, and the tax could be imposed on all earnings. Because the rate is the same for both low earners and high earners, however, the tax bite would soon become too deep for some employees. As for the employer's share, there is no doubt that too high a payroll tax can inhibit employment, creating serious problems for the economy and the society; this may already have happened in some countries of Western Europe. The tax rate, then, cannot be raised indefinitely without such adverse consequences as depressing workers' wages, enlarging the off-the-record economy and decreasing the total tax revenues collected.

Is there some other way to enlarge Social Security revenues? One good opportunity, which should be pursued aggressively, is to bring into the system as many as possible of the workers in government and in nonprofit institutions who are not now included. Uncovered groups make up about 10 percent of the work force. Perhaps workers currently covered by state and local plans could not be compelled to join the system, but Congress could certainly extend coverage to all federal employees. Complex adjustments would be needed to protect the interests of such employees; the difficulties are formidable but not insurmountable. Many experts on the Social Security system advocate starting such a program of consolidation soon, arguing that no other system affords workers and their dependents as broad a range of basic benefits. The National Commission on Social Security has calculated that universal coverage would add an average of $5 billion per year to the revenues of the system over the next 75 years. Of course, it would also increase liabilities.

As for expenditures, is there any equitable way the system's future obligations might be significantly reduced? There is. A growing consensus among those who have studied the system in recent years holds that the standard age of retirement should be increased from 65 to 68. The change would be doubly effective in that it would augment the population of taxpayers while reducing the population of beneficiaries. It should be done only after adequate warning and gradually, perhaps at the rate of only a few months per year. The National Commission estimates that the change would save about $11 billion per year from 1980 to 2055.

The system now tends to promote early retirement. A worker can retire at 62 and get only 20 percent less per year than he would have received at 65. As a result about three in four workers retire before they reach 65. President Reagan proposed changing the early-retirement reduction to 45 percent but withdrew the plan when it met vigorous public opposition.

The increase in early retirement is paralleled by increasing unwillingness of most people to work beyond age 65. Whereas one man in three and one woman in 10 worked after the statutory retirement age in 1960, only one man in five and one woman in 12 does so now. This decline in labor-force participation, combined with increases in longevity, generates pressure on the system. In 1940 only 583 men per 1,000 and 687 women per 1,000 lived to be 65; today the proportions have risen respectively to 711 and 839 per 1,000. Of all people 65 or over fewer than a third were over 75 in 1974; by the end of the century the fraction will be close to a half.

As I indicated above, any increase in the retirement age would have to be phased in gradually. Rita R. Campbell of the Hoover Institution at Stanford University has suggested that allowances might be made for workers who have been employed continuously for as long as 45 years; many private pension plans, she points out, consider the number of years worked as well as age in determining the time of retirement. Furthermore, many people have health problems that make it inadvisable for them to keep working beyond their early sixties, particularly if the job is physically demanding; the definition of disability might be modified to cover such cases.

One alternative to raising the retirement age (or perhaps a companion measure) would be to adopt a recent Swedish approach called phased retirement. Older people can choose a shortened or gradually declining work week instead of going from full-time employment to full retirement in one day.

Might it be possible to limit the increase in the obligations of the Social Security system by shifting some of the burden to alternative sources of income for retired people? Last year the President's Commission on Pension Policy recommended that a compulsory system of private pensions be established. Employers would pay an amount equal to 3 percent of their payroll; changes in tax policy would ease the burden on small businesses. The commission also urged that the tax structure be modified in ways calculated to encourage personal saving.

There is little likelihood that a compulsory private pension plan will be approved by Congress. For one thing, there is continuing mistrust of existing private plans; although Congress attempted in 1974 to regularize such plans and expand their coverage, many workers are still left either without a pension or with a very small one. Private pension plans already cost the U.S. about $15 billion per year in lost tax revenues. Owners of small businesses, many of whom operate close to the margin of profitability, would oppose a compulsory plan bitterly. Effective social control over the reserves of large private pension funds is already a problem; a new program would exacerbate it. Moreover, what is the point of a new compulsory system if the present compulsory system—Social Security—can be made to work?

Many economists contend that the level of personal saving in the U.S. is too low and that this accounts in large part for a deficiency in capital that will have to be remedied if the country is to modernize its plant and equipment. (Martin S. Feldstein of Harvard University undertook some years ago to demonstrate that the Social Security system is directly responsible for the low level of savings, but many economists think he is wrong.) Whether or not additional saving is needed to provide adequate capital for industry (and some economists, including Thomas Juster of the University of Michigan, contest that assumption), Congress has already provided tax advantages for individuals who save for their retirement; the Keogh Plan and the individual retirement account (IRA) are two examples.

Additional tax incentives to encourage more people to save for retirement will probably be forthcoming, but only upper-income people can take full advantage of such opportunities. Any serious attempt to get middle- and low-income groups to divert more of their earnings into savings might require government subvention and protection against inflation for small savers, as is done in Germany. In any case, except for the very poor, private pensions and personal savings already contribute between a fourth and a third of the income of older people. That fraction is unlikely to be raised by more than a few percentage points. There is no alternative, then, to ensuring the financial integrity of the Social Security system so that it can provide basic income for older people.

To accomplish that, it seems to me, the following actions are needed. The Social Security system should be expanded as quickly as possible in order to provide universal coverage, which would add significantly to revenues and also broaden the range of benefits for people now outside the system. An early decision should be made to raise the retirement age gradually, probably to 68. The half of benefits that was based on income and that was never taxed should be made subject to the income tax, but only for those older people whose total income is high enough to make them liable to the tax. It must be determined what changes in Medicare would enable it to provide an acceptable level of medical care for the elderly and to do so more efficiently. The unconscionable inequities imposed on women as workers and as wives should start to be redressed. The benefits for long-service, low-wage workers, which have been adjusted in the recent past, need further adjustment to bring them above the poverty line.

The Social Security system can provide basic support for all older Americans, but only if it is not overloaded. That is why the key reform is to encourage people to work longer, thereby ensuring a comfortable income when they stop working. That is a sensible national goal, and not only for economic reasons. As the Talmud puts it: When you stop working, you are dead.

SOCIAL SECURITY BENEFITS SHOULD BE TAXED[4]

In 1977 the Social Security Retirement Fund was found to be underfinanced by an incredible $4.7 trillion! For that reason, a frightened Congress, late in 1977 after bitter battle, enacted huge payroll tax increases in an attempt to return the system to solvency.

But taxpayers protested the hike in Social Security taxes so loudly that the 1978 income tax cut had to be enacted to make the Social Security levy seem less painful. Meantime, however, basic Social Security reforms continue to await action.

Policymakers now realize that Social Security must be considered as a part of the vast system of government income transfer programs that began in New Deal days and expanded tremendously in the turbulent 1960s.

Income transfers are government payments to individuals whose income is considered insufficient for various reasons. Thus, we have Social Security for the retired, unemployment insurance for the jobless, and welfare for the poor. In fact, a study by the Institute for Socioeconomic Studies discloses

[4] Reprint of newspaper article by Leonard M. Greene, president, Institute for Socioeconomic Studies. *Christian Science Monitor*. Ap. 18, '79. By permission of the publisher and the author.

that as of 1977 there were 182 federal programs for income maintenance and "to fight poverty." Their cost: an astounding $248.1 billion.

The basic flaw in this system of income transfer is its lack of integration. Program has been added on top of program for 40 years. Benefits are repeatedly duplicated.

Social Security, the largest of the income transfers is usually—although incorrectly—thought of as an insurance program. Workers are perceived as "contributors" during their active years who draw on their equity to pay for their retirement benefits.

In actuality, however, Social Security tax payments go directly to retirees now receiving Social Security benefits. It is because the proportion of retirees relative to the active workers actually paying into the system has grown so rapidly in recent years that Social Security has tottered on the brink of bankruptcy.

Another drain on the system has been caused by the fact that Social Security is designed to redistribute income. When low-income workers retire, they receive a larger proportion of their past wages as Social Security benefits than do retirees who earned high wages. Also, a minimum benefit guarantees a pension floor of $121.80 per month at age 65 regardless of past earnings, if the retiree had at least been employed for a minimum amount of time.

In addition to these special benefits for low-income retirees, another program, Supplemental Security Income (SSI), was added in 1974 to supplement the incomes of the aged poor.

Social Security, like much of the rest of the income transfer system, has built-in features that discourage people from working. This problem is particularly acute now that mandatory retirement before age 70 has been prohibited by law.

A recent Harris poll shows that over half of Americans would like to continue working full or part-time after 65. And, our lagging economy could certainly use the productivity of experienced older workers. But the Social Security system continues to penalize any older person who seeks to work. His earnings are taxed twice, first by the IRS and then by Social Security, which deducts $1 in benefits for each $2 (over $4,500) earned by a covered worker between 65 and 72.

Making Social Security payments and other government benefits taxable income would actually be a sound first step toward strengthening national work incentives. If America is going to continue to be guided by the work ethic, it makes no sense to be taxing earnings, while allowing "benefits" to escape tax free. There is no reason to enhance the attractiveness of income that does not require work by also making it tax free!

Subjecting Social Security to taxation would not be prejudicial to low-income retirees. In fact, they would not be in any way affected: there is no income tax liability for the first $7,400 of income for a married couple when both are over 65.

Today the only beneficiaries of a "tax-free" Social Security system are upper-income people who can well afford the minimal tax increase that this proposal would entail. Many of these retirees profit from the loophole that exempts unearned income (interest, dividends, etc.) from benefit reduction.

While taxing Social Security benefits might seem likely to provoke considerable opposition, I foresee little difficulty. The concept of taxing Social Security benefits has been embraced by many advocates of the aging, including Nelson Cruikshank, Counsellor to the President on Aging, who favors it to a limited extent.

Coupled with the elimination of the retirement earnings test, taxation of Social Security benefits will allow senior citizens to pursue their goals—working or leisure—without being pressured by the relative tax disadvantages of working during the golden years.

A SLASH AT SOCIAL SECURITY[5]

In crafting his delicate package of budget cuts, Ronald Reagan carefully corralled a herd of "sacred cows"—Veterans Administration disability benefits and Medicare payments for the elderly, among other programs—that he vowed not to touch. . . . in a move that ensured debate for months to come, the President proposed to chop away at perhaps the most sacred of all cows: Social Security benefits. The plan not only ignited protests from senior citizens' groups around the nation, but finally gave the badly bruised Democrats in Congress a battle they could enthusiastically join—and perhaps stand a good chance of winning. Proclaimed House Speaker Tip O'Neill: "I will be fighting this every inch of the way, and I hope that will be the position of every member of my party."

The proposals, as unveiled by Secretary of Health and Human Services Richard S. Schweiker at a press conference, would entail little reduction in monthly payments for the 36 million Americans already on the rolls or for those who join them before December 31. Administration officials nevertheless calculate that the program of adjustments could save the Treasury about $9 billion in fiscal 1982 and an accumulated total of about $46 billion by 1987. Highlights of the plan:

—Workers who choose early retirement (between the ages of 62 and 65) after 1981 would get only 55 percent of the benefits they would have received at age 65, rather than the 80 percent mandated by current law. Those who retire at 62 next year, for example, would receive an average of $126 a month less than the $372 currently collected. Benefits would also be scrapped for children of early retirees (offspring under 18, or under 22 if they are still in school, are now eligible for payments).

—The formula for calculating initial benefits for those

[5] Reprint of magazine article, by James Kelly, writer. *Time.* 117:24–5. My. 25, '81. Copyright 1981 Time Inc. Reprinted by permission.

who retire at 65 or over after 1982 would be jiggered downward over the next five years. The average worker retiring in 1987, for example, would get $719 a month under the present law, but would receive only $691.90 under Reagan's proposal.

—Beginning in 1982, the annual cost of living increase in benefits, which is based on the Consumer Price Index, would be paid out in October rather than July each year. Based on a projected inflation rate of approximately 8 percent, this three-month delay would save the government about $3 billion in fiscal 1982.

—Under present law those who still work after 65 have their benefits cut by $1 for every $2 they earn over $5,500 a year. To encourage people to work longer, the Administration proposes lifting the ceiling to $10,000 in 1983, $15,000 in 1984, $20,000 in 1985 and then abolishing it completely in 1986.

—Federal and some state employees who are not covered by Social Security are now permitted to retire from their government jobs, work in positions covered by Social Security for a few years and then draw these benefits as well as their government pensions. The Administration proposes reducing Social Security benefits for these "double dippers" by taking their pensions into account.

—Disabled workers would be declared eligible for benefits only for strictly defined medical reasons; age, education and work experience would not be considered. Workers would also have to prove they had not been able to hold a job for 24 months prior to receiving payments rather than just twelve months, and would have to wait six months instead of five before collecting benefits.

To sweeten the medicine of the benefit cuts, Schweiker pointed out that the savings might eventually snip the payroll tax rate levied on employers and employees alike from a projected 7.15 percent in 1986 to 7.05 percent. A worker in his 20s might thus shave about $33,600 off his contribution to the Social Security system by the time he retires at age 65.

Administration officials insisted that the proposals are needed to salvage a system that is teetering on bankruptcy.

Created in 1935, the Social Security Administration originally paid benefits only to workers who retired at age 65; coverage was gradually broadened to include wives, children, the disabled and early retirees. In addition, payments were hiked by cost of living increases. With a negligible inflation rate and a high ratio of taxpaying workers to beneficiaries, the system hummed along smoothly and solvently for decades. In the 1970s, however, prices (which determine the level of payments) rose at a faster clip than wages (which determine how much money is paid into the system). As a result, Social Security funds were depleted at a much faster rate than ever anticipated.

Without some kind of immediate reform, the system could run out of money as early as 1982. Contrary to popular assumption, the Social Security system was never constructed on the basis that what a worker paid in over his lifetime financed his own retirement checks; those working are instead paying for those who have retired. That design will suffer worse strains to come. In the early years of the 21st century, actuaries estimate, there will be only three American workers for every retired person, compared with five for every retiree today; so the system could go bust all over again. Declared Schweiker: "We're trying to stop the old lady from having no check at all."

But those words were of small comfort to the elderly and their supporters across the country. "I think it's outrageous," said Lillian Pasquale, 75, of Miami. "Reagan is picking on the elderly. We're all going to end up in the poorhouse." Both the 50,000-member Gray Panthers and the American Association of Retired Persons have denounced the plan, and local groups are mobilizing to stage rallies and letter-writing campaigns. Said Frank Manning, director of the Massachusetts Legislative Council for Older Americans: "We feel that now that they have started to amend Social Security they won't stop. We have an uneasy feeling they have tasted blood."

Many fear that the cuts will most deeply hurt those who can least afford them. "Over 50 percent of all the people who retired on Social Security do not have private pensions," argues Frank Cassell, 64, a professor of industrial relations at Northwestern University. "That means whatever cuts turn out to be made, these people cannot make up in any way."

For those already on the Social Security rolls, the only trimming in benefits will be the delay of the cost of living increase by three months each year. Warns Professor Robert H. Binstock, 45, director of the National Aging Policy Center on Income Maintenance at Brandeis University: "The October 1 delay will impose real hardship on millions of people next summer. The difference of $25 a month can put between 2 million and 3 million people below the poverty line."

Of great concern to many is the planned slash in benefits to those who choose early retirement. Some 70 percent of those who retire do so now before they reach 65—and obviously many who have been planning to do so in 1982 will have to think twice about leaving their jobs. Others point out that many retire early for health reasons, and they will be unfairly penalized.

The real battle over Reagan's proposed cuts will, of course, be waged in Congress, and the perception there among members of both parties is that the Administration has blundered. "They threw a life rope to Tip O'Neill," quipped Republican Senator Robert Dole of Kansas. The Democrats lost no time in launching their verbal offensive. "We'll find a way to make absolutely certain that the [Social Security] trust fund is actuarially sound, but we're not going to cut benefits," vowed House Democratic Majority Leader Jim Wright of Texas. "That's sneaky."

Many Republicans are also unhappy with Reagan's proposals, if only because they now draw attention away from the President's tax bill. "This ought to have come about the time we finished the tax package, so as not to stir up all the bees at once," complains Dole. But others in the Administration have hopes that some sort of bipartisan approach toward salvaging the Social Security system can be worked out—and that now is the best time to do so. Though White House Chief of Staff James Baker initially opposed pushing for the reforms until after the tax bill was voted upon, OMB Director David

Stockman, Schweiker and others argued convincingly that
the best time to tackle a program as politically sensitive as
Social Security was when the President was riding high in the
polls, as Reagan is now [May '81].

The timing of the announcement was based on a promise
that Schweiker had made to Democratic Representative J. J.
Pickle of Texas, chairman of the House Ways and Means subcommittee that oversees Social Security. The Secretary had
pledged that the Administration would make public its proposals before Pickle's subcommittee began work . . . on its
own bill to reform the system. Pickle, in turn, sounds remark-
ably receptive to striking a deal. "I'm taking the attitude that
the President has made his proposal," he says. "Let's look at it
and see if there might be some compromise. The important
thing is we must pass a bill."

To be sure, the Administration probably acted too swiftly
in putting together and announcing its recommendations.
Reagan had less than one day to review and approve the proposals before Schweiker announced them at his press conference. No advance briefings were held, no public relations
work was done to prepare the public for the cuts, and the Republican leaders of the House and Senate learned of the recommendations only hours before Schweiker's conference.
The aura of haste surrounding the announcement was height-
ened by reports that Stockman wanted to delay the cost of
living increases from July to October this year, rather than in
fiscal 1982, as Schweiker had announced.

Administration officials now say they are willing to listen
to alternative ideas. Presidential Counsellor Edwin Meese, for
example, acknowledged last week at a White House meeting
that the Administration should consider phasing in the penal-
ties against early retirees over several years, rather than im-
posing them at once. Yet the Reaganauts also remain steadfast
in their commitment to achieve long-term solvency for the
Social Security system and believe they will succeed. "The
politics of Social Security have changed," says one White
House aide. Just what changes are actually acceptable will be

revealed in the months ahead as the debate over how to reform the system heats up.

CHANGES TO EXPECT IN YOUR
SOCIAL SECURITY[6]

Americans face unsettling shifts in their retirement benefits as the struggle to strengthen the ailing Social Security system gathers steam.

In a historic turnabout from years of ever more generous
payments, tens of millions of workers and their families may
be forced to put off retirement until later than planned and
accept benefits smaller than expected.

That is what shapes up regardless of which of an array of
plans for saving Social Security finally emerges from the debate now erupting in Washington.

In prospect are smaller monthly payments for future retirees, reduced cost-of-living adjustments for current retirees,
curtailed benefits for dependents and incentives to keep people working longer.

The controversy over how to get Social Security back on a
stable financial course came to a head May 12 when the Reagan Administration unveiled its proposed salvage plan. The
White House wants it to take almost full effect next January.

Key points of the Reagan blueprint:

—Sharply reduced benefits for people who retire before
age 65.

—Lower initial benefits for new retirees at any age.

—A lower ceiling on the maximum family benefits for future retirees.

—Tighter eligibility rules for future recipients of disability payments.

[6] Reprint of staff-written magazine article. *U.S. News & World Report*. 90:26–8.
My. 25, '81. Copyright 1981, U.S. News & World Report, Inc.

—A curb on double dipping by some ex-federal workers who get pensions from both Social Security and the government's civil-service system.

Sweetening the brew is a plan that by 1986 could let Social Security recipients age 65 and over earn as much outside income as they can without losing benefits and an administration promise of lower Social Security taxes in coming years if all goes well.

Administration officials insisted President Reagan is sticking to his campaign promise to maintain benefits for retirees now on Social Security. "These proposals do not remove from the rolls, or cut benefits for, those currently receiving benefits," emphasized Health and Human Services Secretary Richard S. Schweiker.

The one exception is a proposed delay in the annual cost-of-living adjustment to benefits from July's check to October's, starting next year. That's a volatile issue that congressional sources say could face a stiff fight. The administration dropped the idea of attempting the delay this year.

One Step Further

The latest Reagan plan, which is projected to save 46 billion dollars during the five-year period 1982–86, is in addition to other cutbacks in Social Security proposed earlier as part of trimming the federal budget.

Those earlier proposals, which were expected to save an additional 35.5 billion over five years, include an end to benefits for college students, elimination of the $122 floor under monthly Social Security payments, a tighter cap on disability payments and limits on the payment of a current $255 lump-sum amount for funeral expenses.

The White House proposals, says Secretary Schweiker, would keep the Social Security system "from going broke" and put the program "on sound financial ground indefinitely."

Behind the immediate crisis is a projected deficit of 29.1 billion dollars in 1980–84 in the old-age, survivors and disabil-

ity-insurance trust funds. In the long term, an aging population will mean relatively fewer workers to support ever more
retirees if the pace of retirement isn't slowed.

Nevertheless, opposition to benefit cuts is exploding.

"Cutting back on benefits will undermine people's faith in
the integrity of the whole system—they will feel double-
crossed," says Wilbur J. Cohen, a former Secretary of Health,
Education and Welfare and now a leader of Save Our Security, a coalition fighting Social Security cutbacks. One of his
alternatives is to use general tax revenues to help fund the
Medicare part of Social Security, freeing more Social Security
tax revenue for other programs.

The White House acknowledged that mail and phone
calls from the public were running heavily against its plan.

On Capitol Hill, the makings of a political uproar are evident. Speaker of the House Thomas P. "Tip" O'Neill, Jr. (D-
Mass.) called the Reagan plan "despicable" and "a rotten
thing to do." He said that as leader of the Democrats he
would be "fighting this every inch of the way."

Even some Republicans are uneasy. Representative Car-
roll Campbell, who was Reagan's 1980 campaign manager in
South Carolina, urged the administration to take a second
look at its proposals or count on facing a congressional fight
"from within their own ranks, which I may help lead."

Others question whether the President is going far enough.
They urge, among other things, a rise in the normal Social Security retirement age beyond the current 65 and a slowing in
benefit boosts for current retirees.

"You can't say you've dealt with the problem until you
raise the retirement age and also begin to deal with the increasing costs of Medicare," said A. Haeworth Robertson, a
former Social Security official and now a private-employe-
benefits consultant.

Already getting support in the House and Senate are alternative proposals to balance Social Security's books. But
even the most widely backed countermeasures to the Reagan
plan would require sacrifices, including some by people who
are already on the Social Security rolls.

One plan, pushed by Representative J. J. Pickle (D-Tex.), chairman of the House Social Security Subcommittee, would among other things gradually boost the standard retirement age to 68, to be phased in over a 10-year period beginning in 1990.

Revised Base?

Holding favor in the Senate is a plan to slow the annual cost-of-living adjustment for benefits. It would base the adjustment either on rising prices or rising average wages, whichever is lower in a particular year.

For now, the focus of attention has shifted to the package being offered by the White House.

The part of Reagan's plan that would most affect many people's retirement plans is the sharp cut in benefits for persons who retire before age 65. More than 6 out of 10 workers now do that, according to latest estimates.

The administration's goal is to discourage early claims for benefits and at the same time cut the cost of payments to people who still want to retire early. People who work longer also help Social Security's finances by continuing to pay Social Security tax on their earnings.

Currently, people retiring at age 62 get 20 percent less than they would if they were 65. Under Reagan's plan, 62-year-olds would get 45 percent less. People who retire at 63 would get 30 percent less than full benefits instead of today's 13 percent, and 64-year-olds would get 15 percent less instead of 7 percent. The administration also proposes use of a new formula that would lower the age-65 benefit on which early-retirement payments are computed.

Based on government projections, a typical worker who could now count on getting $372.80 a month by retiring at age 62 next January would instead get $246.80, or $126 less. In 1987, the average worker retiring at 62 would get $348.30, about $232 less than under the rules now. A worker at the top level of Social Security would lose $159 a month by retiring early in 1982 and almost $326 by retiring early in 1987.

Nonworking wives who claim benefits at 62 would have them pared from 37½ percent of their husband's age-65 benefits to 27½ percent. Children of those who retired early would no longer get benefits.

Not affected would be spouses of deceased workers. They could continue to collect their benefits as early as age 60 at current levels.

It's the suddenness of the change on early retirement that bothers many critics. Representative Richard Gephardt (D-Mo.) says it "breaks a promise" to many people who have been counting on early retirement.

Senior-citizen groups are also lining up against the proposal. Betty Duskin, director of research for the National Council of Senior Citizens, says many people retire early not because they want to but because of health problems, failure to find jobs or inability to keep up with strenuous work.

Against such opposition, Reagan, at this point, is seen as likely to have to settle for a gradual phase-in of tougher early-retirement rules.

One result of the proposal could be to force a decision on people who turn 62 this year and have been contemplating early retirement. If the Reagan plan passes, these people would come out much better by getting on Social Security before the changes start.

Generating less of an immediate uproar, but of growing importance for the future, is a proposal to adjust the way in which initial benefits are determined. The benefit is based on a retiree's past wages, which now are upgraded to better correspond with today's wage standards. The White House, however, claims that recent retirees have been overcompensated.

The administration's proposed new formula would mean lower monthly benefits in the future for people who retire at any age. For example, a worker with average pay who can now expect to get $719 a month at age 65 in 1987 would, under Reagan's plan, get just under $692. At the top wage level for Social Security, a worker would get almost 9 percent less.

Almost half the long-term savings in the Reagan plan over the next 75 years would come from this change.

Another group facing loss of benefits under the Reagan program would be persons who claim disability benefits.

The waiting period for benefits to start would be increased from five to six months, a disability would be expected to last at least 24 months instead of 12, and a determination ,of disability could be based only on medical considerations without taking into consideration age, education or occupational problems, as at present. Also, in the 10 years before disability most workers must have been employed for at least 30 quarters, instead of only 20 as now. This is another area in which opposition may force a compromise.

Offering a Carrot

One way Reagan hopes to dull opposition to his Social Security cuts is by holding out the carrot of lower payroll taxes to support the program.

The levy, now 6.65 percent of covered earnings, is scheduled to rise gradually to 7.65 percent by 1990. The administration says that if its plans work out the rate could be cut to 6.45 percent and held there between 1985 and 2019. The wage base upon which the tax is levied, now $29,700, would still grow as wage levels rise. The White House says a young person starting work next year could save $33,600 in taxes over a lifetime under its proposal.

Another Reagan idea designed to offset criticism is the proposal to remove by 1986 the lid on what a person 65 or over can earn without giving up benefits. Now, someone aged 65 to 71 loses $1 of benefits for every $2 of earnings above $5,-500. The lid goes to $6,000 in 1982 and Reagan would increase it to $10,000 in 1983, $15,000 in 1984 and $20,000 in 1985 before having it phased out in 1986. People who retire early would again be penalized. They would remain under the present system of limits.

One effect of removing the earnings lid would be to make Social Security less of a retirement program and more of an annuity. A person could continue to work full time at his or her old job and still collect benefits. "That's something you don't see in private pensions," says one consultant.

Advisers say the assault on Social Security benefits will force individuals to be more self-reliant. "People will have to do more saving and investment on their own," says George Barbee of the Consumer Financial Institute in Newton, Mass.

Bracing for another kind of impact are firms with their own pension plans. Many of these plans are geared to provide a set share of a worker's pay, less a deduction for Social Security benefits. If benefits slip, employers may be required to make up the difference. Even where there is no link with Social Security, employers will come under pressure to sweeten their plans as Social Security benefits dip.

Whatever finally shapes up, it is clear that people of all ages will have to reassess what Social Security will bring them in the future.

CUTS IN SOCIAL SECURITY[7]

With 3 million Americans set to lose their social-security checks . . . [last] March unless Congress changes its mind, the atmosphere in a House hearing room . . . was predictably tense. Spokesmen for the Reagan administration argued that many of those scheduled to lose the $122 minimum monthly benefit were actually retired federal workers with comfortable pensions—or homemakers supported by their spouses—and that all but about 140,000 would be adequately cared for by other government-assistance programs. That sunny position came under immediate attack. House Social-Security subcommittee chairman J. J. Pickle, 67, angrily challenged the Administration's statistics. Congressional Budget Office director Alice Rivlin reported that many of those losing the meager benefit would be women or retirees over 80 years old.

[7] Reprint of staff-written magazine article. *Newsweek.* 98:40. S. 21, '81. Copyright 1980 by Newsweek Inc. All rights reserved. Reprinted by permission.

And Representative Frank J. Guarini of New Jersey asked plaintively, "Is this truly a humane thing for the government to do?"

The current battle over the minimum benefit, eliminated in the omnibus budget bill this summer, is only a minor skirmish in the full-scale war over Social Security that faces the Reagan administration this fall. Unless reforms are made, the system's basic retirement fund could temporarily run dry around Election Day next year, and the problems will multiply when the baby-boom generation retires early next century. But the struggle to change the system is intensely political—America's elderly vote in large numbers and are likely to view any benefit cuts as a breach of trust. Still smarting from the Senate's 96–0 rejection of its initial reform ideas last May, the Administration plans to keep a nervous distance from the deliberations this time. But the time to enact major revisions—before the 1982 campaign begins "is running out," warns Health and Human Services Secretary Richard Schweiker. "We all realize that it will be impossible to do it next year."

Strategy

On the advice of Republican strategists, the White House has sent no further suggestions to Capitol Hill. "We told them not to send us *anything*," said one GOP Senate staffer. But Reagan's agenda is clear—and only slightly less wrenching than his spurned May proposals. Aides still hope to trim the system's swelling expenditures by tightening eligibility requirements for the disabled, reducing "double dipping" by retired federal workers (who qualify for separate pensions), changing the formulas that determine initial-benefit levels and cutting benefits for workers who retire early (at age 62)—though more gradually than the immediate 31 percent cut proposed by Reagan last spring. At a GOP strategy meeting last week, Reagan suggested phasing in the early-retirement cuts over two or three years; Senate Majority Leader Howard Baker and House Minority Leader Robert Michel warned that it would have to be even more gradual.

The unenviable task of drafting legislation that will solve the system's fiscal problems and still win bipartisan support falls to the Senate Finance Committee, chaired by Robert Dole. He hopes to have a compromise bill written by mid-October, but must first sort through the pet proposals of other GOP leaders. Social-Security subcommittee chairman William Armstrong, for example, has favored raising the retirement age by one month per year until it reaches 68. Senate Budget Committee chairman Pete Domenici has suggested limiting the annual cost-of-living adjustment (COLA)—$16 billion this year—to 3 percent less than the rise in the consumer price index. These two concepts were not part of the Administration's May proposals, but Reagan aides say the President might buy them. And limiting the COLA has one key virtue: it is favored by the Senate Finance Committee's ranking Democrat, Russell Long of Louisiana.

The support of Long and Daniel P. Moynihan, ranking minority member of the Senate Social-Security panel, is crucial to a bipartisan package. But Moynihan contends the system is basically sound and needs only minor reforms. Last week he proposed a bill that would allow the system's various funds simply to borrow from one another to cover shortfalls. He also favors granting the system stand-by authority to dip into general-revenue funds—a position Reagan opposes. Clearly, hammering out a compromise will not be easy, but Dole has so far won good marks for his cheerful efforts to reach a consensus. "At first I thought about coming up with a 'Dole proposal'," he deadpanned. "But upon reflection, I realized that it would be better if it was a 'Dole-Moynihan-Long proposal'."

Achilles' Heel

Winning support in the House will be more difficult. Many Democratic leaders there share Moynihan's faith in the system and intend to offer little cooperation on the politically treacherous issue. "I think we should request that the Administration send up its program and then give it every opportunity for public debate," said Ways and Means Democrat Ken Holland with a sly grin. Democratic leaders are so gleeful about the prospect of Reagan's proposals becoming a GOP Achilles' heel during the 1982 campaigns that they are quietly discouraging Representative Pickle's yearlong efforts to suggest his own Social-Security reforms. "[Reagan] wants somebody else to break his commitment on Social Security—why should we be the ones?" asks one Democrat. "Politics is rampant in this place right now," says another staffer.

With 36 million Americans depending on Social Security and millions more worried about its fate, according to recent polls, the politicization of reform was inevitable. This week the American Federation of State, County and Municipal Employees (AFSCME) will begin airing TV ads attacking the Administration's approach. "Why, the government acts as though they're giving us a handout," says the indignant wife of a retiree in the ad. But unpopular as the reforms may be, the system's problems remain real and acute, as even some Democrats privately admit. The danger is that too many lawmakers will be reluctant to prescribe the bad-tasting medicine—and that later the illnesses of the system will be far more difficult to cure.

BIG DEFICITS FOR SOCIAL SECURITY, SMALL CHANCE FOR REFORM[8]

It is true that if the Social Security system can somehow stay afloat through the '80s, it will sail into calmer waters for a long period beginning around 1990. For one thing, a 1 percent tax increase—half a point each on workers and employers—goes into effect that year. For another, the number of people retiring from 1990 through the rest of the century will

    [8] Magazine article by George J. Church, contributor. *Time*. 118:16–27. My. 24, '82. Copyright 1982 by Time Inc. All rights reserved. Reprinted by permission.

be held down by the low birth rates of the Depression and World War II years. Meanwhile, members of the 1946–1964 baby-boom generation will be hard at work, presumably earning rising incomes and paying swelling Social Security taxes, even without a further increase. The ratio of workers paying into the system to people drawing benefits, after falling from 16.5 to 1 in 1950 to 3.2 to 1 now, will at last stabilize at about the current level. Says Alicia Munnell, vice president of the Federal Reserve Bank of Boston and a leading Social Security authority: "We go through the '90s in great, great shape." Assuming we can get to the '90s.

There is no excuse for complacency, as Munnell also points out, since the prosperity of the '90s will affect only the pension and disability funds. The Medicare fund could be bare by 1990 and draining reserves out of the other two. At least, that is likely if hospital costs keep climbing as rapidly as they have been doing for the past several decades (in March, while the CPI as a whole went down for the first time in 17 years, its medical-care component went right on increasing at a 12 percent annual rate).

The real long-range worry is a potential demographic disaster for Social Security, beginning around the year 2010. Then the baby boomers will start to retire, in numbers greater than U.S. society has ever had to cope with. Meanwhile, the working population will have been thinned by the low birth rates of the past 15 years. The ratio of Social Security taxpayers to beneficiaries, after holding at about 3 to 1 into the early 21st century, could drop to as low as 2 to 1 by 2030. According to some projections, the Social Security taxes that those two workers and their employers would have to pay to support one retired person could drain away 25 percent of American payrolls. That would not only put an all but unbearable strain on the 21st century economy, but could provoke a tax rebellion among the young. Warns Michael J. Boskin, an economist and Social Security expert at Stanford University: "This could cause the greatest polarization in the U.S. since the Civil War. It would be age warfare."

No such doomsday scenario is inevitable. It could be

changed by a renewed surge in birth rates, for example, or a continued rise in immigration by Hispanics and Asians, most of whom are young and who will work and pay Social Security taxes for many years before they collect benefits.

But it would be most imprudent to stall on fundamental reform of the Social Security system and trust to these uncertainties. As Boskin puts it, if pessimistic demographic predictions come true and "we wait until early next century to do something about this, the Social Security deficit could be well over a trillion dollars." Given the moral imperative of providing people who are now working with ample time to adjust their retirement plans to changes in Social Security, the Administration and Congress should combine action to ease the immediate cash squeeze and budget deficit with long-range reforms, legislated now to take effect gradually over the decades. Otherwise, the prosperous '90s might be no more than an interlude between crises.

There is no dearth of plans for both short- and long-range reform. Experts have exhaustively debated dozens of proposals; it seems most unlikely that the Greenspan commission can come up with any new ones. What has been lacking, and is still lacking, is the political will to overcome the furious opposition that a proposed change in Social Security inevitably arouses.

Short Term Solutions

The one solution that gets very little discussion is any raising of Social Security payroll taxes still further, on top of the huge future increases already written into law. Though some Social Security experts believe that a relatively small additional increase could both stop the immediate cash drain and build adequate reserves to handle the 21st century demographic dilemma, the idea makes politicians shudder. As a matter of equity and politics, there is little appeal in further increasing a tax whose burden falls most heavily on low-income workers, while the well off escape Social Security taxes on a portion of their earnings and are having their income taxes cut. There is justified concern too that another payroll-tax boost could further delay the economic recovery that would help Social Security more than anything.

That leaves two general classes of short-term solutions:

TAP GENERAL REVENUES

Liberals, and others opposed to any reduction in benefits, argue for using income tax and other revenues to make any payments that cannot be financed by the payroll tax. Former Social Security Commissioner Robert M. Ball contends that the system could get through the '80s with relatively small "borrowings," which could be repaid, with interest, out of the reserves that the pension fund will again begin to accumulate in the '90s.

The argument against general-revenue financing is stated succinctly by Social Security Commissioner John Svahn: "*What* general revenues?" In an era of budget deficits that could all too easily approach $200 billion a year, the government simply has no funds to spare. Diverting money to Social Security would force the government to borrow even more from the financial markets than it is already doing to finance defense and general social spending, thus helping to keep interest rates high.

Alternatively, giving Social Security an open-ended call on general revenues might prompt further cutbacks in other programs, such as food stamps and Aid to Families with Dependent Children, which the poor need more and which have already been slashed severely. Says Elizabeth Kutza, associate professor at the University of Chicago's School of Social Service Administration: "There is now open competition among welfare groups. There is fear that the elderly will capture all the welfare resources, at the expense of other disadvantaged people" who have no powerful lobby to speak for them. That competition is difficult to mediate, she adds, because "most people now regard Social Security as a guarantee of middle-class income levels. The elderly lobby groups represent a white-collar view of the world."

SLOW THE GROWTH OF BENEFITS

Despite much demagoguery, no one is talking about snipping so much as a penny off present benefits; anyone now receiving an average pension check of $379 a month can count on continuing to collect at least that much, unless the trust funds do indeed run dry. But it seems imperative to keep future inflation from pushing up benefits as rapidly as it did from 1975 to 1981. Besides saving money for the trust funds and helping to trim the overall budget deficit in the short run, a limit on future increases could also help build up reserves to soften the 21st century's demographic crunch. Any increase decreed now will almost certainly be frozen into the benefit rates paid to future retirees; the cumulative cost over the decades is gigantic.

Debates over what to do about Social Security in forthcoming federal budgets initially focused on quick, temporary ways to conserve cash. Among the suggestions: a one-year freeze on cost of living adjustments (COLAS) in Social Security pension benefits and many other federal programs, an idea first put forward in February by Democratic Senator Ernest Hollings of South Carolina, which would save $11.3 billion; and a three-month delay in the COLA that might be paid in July 1983 (estimated savings: $3.3 billion at an 8 percent inflation rate), a plan advanced by Senate Republican Leader Howard Baker in an unsuccessful attempt to keep budget-compromise negotiations between Reagan and congressional leaders from breaking down at the end of April.

To have more than a brief impact on the deficit, any such plan would have to be combined with a cap on future COLAS. One proposal advocated vigorously by Harvard's Martin Feldstein, a member of *Time*'s Board of Economists, would be to limit future increases to "inflation less 2 percent"; that is, if the CPI rose 8 percent in a given year, Social Security benefits would go up only 6 percent. The virtue of this plan is that it would be similar to the treatment of COLAS in private industry: workers whose wages are indexed to inflation generally get raises equal to only a portion of the CPI increase.

The most popular idea among academic experts is to index benefits either to the rise in prices or to the increase in average wages throughout the economy—whichever is less.

That would keep benefits in inflationary periods from racing far ahead of tax collections, which are keyed to the rise in wages. Advocates defend the plan on grounds of equity too: Why should the elderly be afforded fuller protection against the ravages of inflation than the young and middle-aged workers whose taxes pay for their pensions?

Stanford Economist Rita Ricardo-Campbell emphasizes the most damning Social Security statistics of all: since 1970 average Social Security benefits, adjusted for inflation, have risen a remarkable 37 percent; average weekly wages, adjusted for inflation, have not increased at all. Says Ricardo-Campbell: "We have been taking real income from young people who are heads of households, who don't own a home, who don't have the assets, and giving it to the old people," at least some of whom live in mortgage-free homes and who have accumulated savings." Says M.I.T.'s Thorow: "If real wages go up, real Social Security benefits should go up. But if real wages go down, you can't expect the elderly to be immune from all the problems facing the economy."

Public opinion just might be swinging toward some such solution. Harris polls conducted for the National Council on the Aging last year found that 73 percent of those questioned generally opposed reductions in COLAS. Those responding to a March Gallup poll, however, voted narrowly in favor of lower COLAS as part of a general hold-down on federal spending, 48 percent to 44 percent. The trouble for politicians, of course, is that the only people who are likely to vote for or against a candidate on the basis of that one issue are the aged, and they are still passionately opposed to any tampering with COLAS. This opposition is basically driven not by economic calculation but by plain fear of a poverty-ridden old age—and this fear is an understandably powerful motivation. Like many other retired couples, Evan Francis, 75, and his wife Mildred, 77, of Los Angeles, wrongly interpret any talk of lower future benefits as a threat to the $582 a month they receive from Social Security. Says Evan: "If the government cuts it off, there would be a revolution in the streets.

A continuing drop in the inflation rate will of course automatically and painlessly reduce COLAS. As President Reagan observed . . . : "By the time next year rolls around, there maybe won't be any cost of living increase, because there won't be any increase in the cost of living." It would be risky to assume that this happy state will indefinitely continue: there have been too many periods in the past when inflation dwindled, only to flare up again.

For the longer run, the most plausible idea for reforming Social Security is to reverse the trend toward earlier retirement by gradually raising the retirement age at which full benefits are paid. Advocates note that the same advances in medical science and health care that have been lengthening the lives of the retired would also permit them to keep working for more years. Congress recognized this reality in 1978 when it voted to raise the mandatory retirement age from 65 to 70. If the age for collecting full Social Security benefits were raised to 68 from 65, and the early retirement age to 65 from 62, the savings to Social Security would be tremendous.

The key to any attempt to raise the eligibility age, Social Security experts agree, is to phase in any change slowly, giving workers who are now in late or mid-career time to adjust their retirement plans. The central feature of Reagan's disastrous proposals last May was a reduction for those who retire at 62 from 80 percent of full benefits to 55 percent—starting January 1, 1982. The Senators who voted 96 to 0 to oppose his plan protested vehemently that it would be an unconscionable blow to people who had already made plans to retire within the next year.

Texas Democrat J. J. Pickle, chairman of the House Ways and Means Subcommittee on Social Security, at that time was drafting a bill to raise from 65 to 68 the retirement age at which full benefits could be collected, in small steps beginning in 1990 and ending in the year 2000. In one of the more egregious examples of the partisanship that has dogged all efforts at Social Security reform, House Speaker Tip O'Neill ordered Pickle to go no further. The reason: O'Neill saw an opportunity for Democrats to assail Reagan as an enemy of

Social Security, and he did not want the issue clouded by anything that could be interpreted as a Democratic plan to reduce benefits for anybody.

A more reasonable objection to raising the retirement age
is voiced by Harvard Economist William Hsiao. Says he:
"Armchair professors and bureaucrats who sit behind desks
pushing a pencil all day can work until age 68 without any serious difficulty," but manual workers are too worn out by
physical labor to stay on the job that long. Others insist that
many of the people who now retire at 62 do so less because of
choice than because of failing health or inability to find another job if they are laid off in their early 60s. For those reasons, Pickle's bill, while raising the age for full benefits to 68,
would have permitted retirement at 64 percent of normal
benefits at any age after 62.

Other Reforms

Though Pickle's bill has been sidetracked, the idea of de-
laying retirement remains a plausible way to ease the burden
on the system. Beginning this year, Social Security laws offer
a 3 percent increase in eventual retirement benefits for each
year that workers stay on the job past their 65th birthday;
some experts suggest raising that bonus to 8 percent or 10
percent. House Majority Leader James Wright, another Texas
Democrat, talks of substituting income tax credits for each
year of continued employment past age 65.

Some other reform proposals that are worthy of consideration but need more exploration before they can enter the political debate.

—*Tax Social Security benefits.* No one proposes applying
income taxes to the half of benefits that are financed by taxes
levied on employers, but some economists advocate taxing
the half that is financed out of deductions from workers' paychecks. Mickey Levy, in a study done for the American Enterprise Institute, a conservative Washington-based think
tank, calculates that three-fifths of all Social Security beneficiaries would pay no tax anyway, because their incomes are

too low and their exemptions too high (people over 65 get double the current $1,000 personal exemption from income taxes). Taxes paid by the other two-fifths, he figures, could be recycled back into the Social Security system and would not only ease the current cash squeeze but also help build reserves for the future. However, no politician wants to take on the job of explaining to retired people why any of the benefits they regard as a sacred right purchased by past taxes should be subject to a new tax.

—*Cover everybody.* At present, some 3 million federal employees do not contribute to Social Security. They belong to a separate civil service system that gives them higher pensions. Bringing them into Social Security would bolster the system's reserves and also end the "double dipping" that permits federal employees to retire early on a civil service pension, work for a few years in a job in private industry, and qualify for a Social Security pension too. But any proposal for such changes faces two serious obstacles. Federal employees constitute a significant lobbying force, and included in their numbers are Senators and Congressmen, a group not famous for voting against its self-interest—ever.

—*Rewrite benefit formulas.* A change in the complex formulas for calculating benefits, in order to give a newly retired worker an initial pension representing a somewhat lower percentage of what he earned in his last years on the job, could produce large long-run savings. It also would return the Social Security system to Roosevelt's idea of basic minimum protection against poverty, and would prod those now working to save more for their retirement. Encouraging savings is a goal that hardly any economist, conservative or liberal, will quarrel with.

In the end, the solution to Social Security's double dilemma—of an immediate cash crisis and the threat of a long-range demographic disaster—is unlikely to come from any single approach. What is needed is a combination of steps: some immediate limitation on COLAS, some intermediate move to prevent inflation from pushing up benefits faster than the rise in wages and payroll taxes, some long-range measures to raise the retirement age and keep the formula for calculating benefits from straining the resources of society.

The danger is that Congress and the administration will do none of the above. Instead, they are all too likely to let the system drift closer to the point at which the money runs out, then enact a series of emergency proposals—and trust to luck. To change the system so that it can both surmount the current money shortage and continue providing protection to the elderly and disabled without placing an intolerable burden on the young involves making the kind of choices that politicians so far have been running from, with irresponsible cowardice.

Chicago Social Security expert Kutza summarizes the problem: "Everyone knows the range of possible solutions. There has been panel after panel, discussion after discussion; every single option has been documented. The only real question is: "Which political leader is willing to bite that bullet?" The answer right now seems to be nobody, because every suggested solution will offend some powerful group. But the reconciliation of conflicting interests is the real art of politics. In this case, some form of reconciliation is a social necessity.

CONGRESSIONAL ADDRESS BY REPRESENTATIVE J. J. (JAKE) PICKLE[9]

No more important challenge faces this government today than restoring confidence in Social Security. It is so much a part of the financial underpinning of this country and its economy that confidence in Social Security must be viewed on an equal basis with the tax cut and spending budget matters.

[9] Reprint of transcript of speech by Representative J. J. Pickle (Democrat), *Congressional Digest.* 60:210, 212, 214, 216. Ag. / S. '81. Copyright 1981, The Congressional Digest Inc. Reprinted by permission.

The subcommittee has tentatively agreed upon a program which would meet the President's budget targets, although not in the same way he originally proposed. The subcommittee further agreed to consider a proposal aimed at the long-term problems. This proposal would move full retirement to age 68 by the year 2000 while also preserving the option to retire as young as age 62. It also would eliminate the Social Security retirement test at age 68 beginning in 1983.

I am introducing legislation regarding Social Security financing. The bill I am introducing incorporates the 23 concepts tentatively agreed upon in the subcommittee. It also includes a transfer of some funding from the HI—Medicare—fund into the retirement fund to insure adequate money for now and the future. This particular concept, transfer of one-half of the HI revenues to the OASI fund, is one item which has not been agreed to by the subcommittee. We do know we must raise approximately $20 billion a year additional for the next 5 years. I think the transfer of some of the HI funds will be the most likely route to go. The bill meets the President's budget objectives, meets the short-term needs of the system, and provides sufficient funding in the future to meet the system's needs even if current reasonable and normal economic projections do not pan out.

This is the chairman's bill—not a subcommittee bill. I speak in this legislation as one individual member. But I speak as one who is determined to take Social Security out of the headlines and to set the people's minds at ease for decades to come. It is of utmost importance that the Congress meet this challenge. The time to act is now.

There are three Social Security trust funds, maintained separately although all are financed out of the FICA payroll tax: retirement and survivor's insurance, disability insurance, and health insurance.

The Social Security retirement and survivor's trust fund will become unable to pay benefits sometime in mid-1982. Even if the assets of the disability fund were added in, the two funds together would still be insufficient late in 1982. This shortfall is projected under both the Carter administration's fiscal year 1982 budget economic assumptions and the Reagan revised fiscal year 1982 budget assumptions.

If the assets of all three funds, including health insurance, are considered together, the trust funds are adequate to make benefit payments through 1986 under the Reagan economic assumptions, but are insufficient by late in 1984 under the Carter assumptions. Even under the Reagan assumptions, the margin is extremely thin. Assets in all three funds combined drop to only 14 percent or only 1½ months worth of reserves. If economic conditions in the next 3 years are only slightly worse than the Reagan administration predicts, the trust funds will be unable to make benefit payments at some point before 1986.

An additional $110 billion in revenues, or approximately $20 billion a year, likely will be needed to achieve a 25-percent trust fund reserve by 1986.

In addition to the practical problem of providing sufficient revenues to the system, the general public apparently has little confidence in the soundness of the Social Security program. We need to take action now that will restore the public's confidence.

This legislation contains two provisions specifically to insure the fiscal soundness of the trust funds:

Interfund borrowing: This provision allows borrowing among the three trust funds if assets of any one fund fall below 20 percent of 1 year's benefit payments. In this way, shortfalls in one fund, such as the one due to occur in the retirement and survivor's fund in 1982, could be made up for by loans from another fund.

General revenues for HI: Beginning in 1983, an amount equal to one-half the revenues from the present HI tax rate would be paid into the HI trust fund from the general fund of the Treasury. One-half of the HI tax rate would at the same time be reallocated to the OASDI trust funds.

These two provisions combined should guarantee the solvency of the trust funds through the end of the century.

The legislation I am introducing meets the President's budget targets, but through a different route. I reject the concept of changing the minimum benefit in such a way that it would reduce the actual benefits of people who may have been receiving the minimum for some time. This bill would eliminate the minimum benefit—but on a prospective basis only.

Second, I do not think a student's education should be interrupted and have followed an approach whereby those who are now juniors in high school could be assured they would receive their students' benefits. My bill would freeze the students' benefits at their current levels rather than providing for a 25 percent annual reduction and would not pay benefits during June, July, and August to any individual not a full-time summer student. I would further add that I do not think anything should be done regarding the students' benefit if the other assistance programs are not funded to take up the slack.

In accordance with the subcommittee decision, I have included a provision to round Social Security benefits down to the nearest dollar on the final benefit computation.

Also in accordance with the subcommittee decisions, I have included the President's proposals in the disability program for a megacap and for changes in the workman's compensation offset. I have not included the proposals for a stricter insured status requirement for disability or for elimination of the lump-sum death benefit and have altered the elimination of the vocational rehabilitation funding to provide for funding in cases where there is a successful rehabilitation that enables a beneficiary to return to the work force.

Also to meet the budget targets, my bill provides for a direct deposit of State and local FICA taxes with the federal government, and makes other changes.

The bill includes provisions, first, which provide a limited earnings sharing upon divorce for cases in which the marriage lasted at least 25 years before divorce and in which the lower earning spouse is age 50 or over, and, second, which would compute benefits for aged survivors based on the deceased spouses' earnings record indexed by wage changes up to the year in which the worker would have reached age 60 so that when a worker dies long before retirement age the surviving spouse's benefit is not based on earnings several years out of date.

It also includes provisions to eliminate the advantage individuals with pensions from uncovered employment gain from the weighting of the Social Security benefit formula when they have short earnings histories in the Social Security system, and a provision to extend for 5 additional years the current exemption from the government pension offset for certain spouses of covered workers.

Finally, the bill would eliminate the retirement test for individuals age 68 and over beginning in January 1983.

The provisions of this bill will meet the President's budget targets, they will provide financial security for Social Security in the near term, and they will provide a cushion of financing in the long term. The history of the past several years has been that we have tended to be too optimistic about our economic assumptions. Until our experience improves, prudence demands that we take this step.

CONGRESSIONAL ADDRESS BY SENATOR ROBERT J. DOLE[10]

What is the status of the Social Security trust funds? According to a rather sophisticated study recently completed by the Congressional Research Service of the Library of Congress in conjunction with the Office of the Actuary and the Office of Research and Statistics of the Social Security Administration, the combined old age and survivors insurance and disability insurance trust funds will not have sufficient reserves to pay a full month's benefits by the middle of 1982 and reserves could run out completely in 1983. The combined OASI, DI, and hospital insurance trust funds will just barely have sufficient reserves to pay benefits and only if no unex-

[10] Reprint of transcript of speech by Senator Robert J. Dole (Republican). *Congressional Digest.* 60:202, 204, 206. Ag. / S. '81. Copyright 1981, the Congressional Digest Inc. Reprinted by permission.

pected economic problems arise. The magnitude of the problem is very great, but not insurmountable, if we act expeditiously and wisely.

Is the problem severe enough to warrant immediate action? Yes, the 97th Congress must act during its first session to deal with the short-term financing problem since benefit payments cannot otherwise be met. But, in addition to the short-term problem, there is a major long-term financing deficiency in the program. We need to deal with this long-term financing problem at the same time.

Due to the increases in Social Security taxes scheduled over the next several years, once we take care of the immediate shortfall in the Social Security trust funds we should be solvent through the year 2010. At that point, when the baby boom generation begins to retire, we face a very severe financing problem. That problem can be solved by gradual slowing of the rate of growth of the Social Security program. But this kind of solution is possible only if we act now. If we wait until after the turn of the century, the only solutions will be drastic benefit cuts or huge tax increases.

What are the alternatives for solving the financing problems? There are three alternatives. One is to raise taxes, but I do not believe that is an option at this time. I am not even sure we can count on the increases already scheduled under current law.

A second alternative is to provide another source of revenue, such as general fund financing, a value added tax, a special tax on certain products such as tobacco or alcohol. Support for most of these methods has proven very unpopular, even disastrous for some members of Congress. There is also a particular danger in the general revenue financing approach: It removes Social Security benefits from the status of an "earned right" subject only to the eligibility condition that an individual worked in covered employment for a sufficient period of time; therefore, Social Security benefits, whether it be Medicare only, or disability, or all benefits, may become means tested—that is, eligibility will be based on need rather than contribution—and those who have paid in for years may not be eligible for benefits. In particular with general fund financing, any discipline for containing program growth will be lost.

The third alternative, which I support, is to make changes in the program which will contain the rate of growth of program costs.

The final alternative obviously cannot be used to solve the short-term financing problem since it will require time to accomplish real savings. At the same time, I do not believe the Congress will want to make drastic cuts in benefits of individuals currently on the rolls or increase taxes any further. Therefore, we may have to consider some infusion of general funds. That is all the more reason for dealing with the long-term problem at the same time. That way, Congress can get credit for preserving the integrity of the system and insuring solvency of the trust funds in exchange for some less pleasant or desirable short-term solution.

What are my recommendations for curtailing costs? I do not have a specific proposal at this time. However, I do believe there are several broad areas where improvements are possible and which I believe the American people will support.

First, I believe the formula for determining benefits and the average earnings on which benefits are based can be restructured in such a way that benefits can continue to grow but not as fast as they have been growing. Second, I believe we need to identify areas where other government programs have been instituted to provide benefits for similar purposes, such as disability, education, basic income maintenance, or retirement, and determine how to provide a better blend of such programs to ease the burden on Social Security wherever possible. Third, we should find ways to make work more attractive than retirement. Fourth, we should improve the administration of the programs, which we have allowed to deteriorate over the last few years because of the ever-increasing demands on the Social Security Administration to handle other programs, in order to eliminate fraud, abuse and waste wherever it occurs.

A combination of improvements along these lines will provide extensive savings and should allow us to make the program solvent without having to do things like raise the retirement age to 68 or merge the civil service retirement program into Social Security.

Can the private sector do a better job? The most important thing to remember about the Social Security program is that it is a social insurance system. Therefore it carries with it certain social costs. The program has always been designed to balance "social adequacy" against "individual equity." Most often, when people talk about turning the program over to the private sector or eliminating the so-called "welfare aspects" of the program, I think they ignore the social function of the program. I believe we should attempt the improvements outlined before we consider a complete dismantling of the system. I think those improvements will work and I believe we have the support of the American people to enact the necessary reforms.

I just do not believe that we can postpone a solution to the problem another year. It is up to this Congress. We can do certain short-term things, maybe borrow from different funds to get through the short term. But in the long term, we must address the problem.

CONGRESSIONAL ADDRESS BY SENATOR JOSEPH R. BIDEN[11]

On Tuesday, May 12, Secretary Schweiker announced the Administration's plans to severely cut Social Security benefits for millions of Americans. These proposals if enacted would signal a significant retrenchment in America's commitment to her senior citizens. We would be, in effect, changing the rules in the middle of the game for the millions of Americans who

[11] Reprint of transcript of speech by Senator Joseph R. Biden (Democrat). *Congressional Digest.* 60:203, 205, 207. Ag. / S. '81. Copyright 1981, the Congressional Digest Inc. Reprinted by permission.

have regularly and faithfully contributed to the system for years with the expectation that they would get certain benefits under certain conditions.

The draconian nature of these proposals is also unnecessary. Obviously the Social Security system has financial problems and these problems must be solved, but not at the expense of weakening the system's integrity. The Reagan proposals seek to solve this problem in one way: By cutting benefits. But there are other alternatives such as interfund borrowing which, in part, could ease the short-term cash flow problem facing the system now.

I am firmly opposed to the proposal to reduce early retirement benefits beginning January 1. Retirement is not a decision which is made overnight. Most persons plan their retirement 5, 10, or 20 years in advance. Their retirement income is premised on the expectation that they will receive x dollars in benefits. If this benefit is cut by 25 percent as the Administration proposes, then many persons who wanted to retire could not afford to retire or they would incur a substantial drop in the quality of living.

I am also concerned about the Administration's proposals to reduce the replacement ratio from 42 percent to 38 percent of a worker's preretirement earnings. There is nothing sacred about a 42 percent preretirement earnings ratio. Most experts agree that a retiree needs about 67 to 75 percent of his average preretirement earnings in order to maintain the same standard of living. But we have to recognize that Social Security alone cannot meet all the income needs of a senior citizen. It was never intended to be the sole source of retirement income.

The Social Security Administration reported in 1976 that of 17.3 million households aged over 65, 10.6 million relied on Social Security as their sole pension source. Of these 10.6 million, fully one-third lived below the poverty level, even with Social Security benefits.

If you have outside earnings plus your Social Security you may be in good shape. If you have unearned income from stocks and bonds or private pension in addition to your Social

Security you may be alright. These are the types of people who can afford to move to condominiums in Palm Springs or travel to Europe. But for many senior citizens, that Social Security pension is all they have. And although the pension may be indexed to inflation, it was never enough to meet basic day to day living needs.

The Administration says it wants to encourage people to work longer. Included in the Reagan package is a proposal raising the earned income limitation from the present $5,500 in 1981 to $10,000 in 1983 and removing it entirely by 1986. I agree with that policy and I have argued since I came to the Senate that the earned income limitation should be lifted.

But for the older person who is physically unable to work, for the worker who can work at some job but not his present job because of physical limitation and for those elderly facing age discrimination in the job market, the Administration proposals do not help them. They are not enough.

If you are going to say to America's workers that they cannot retire at 62, that Social Security benefits are no longer going to be as generous as they once were, that we will no longer fully protect them against the effects of inflation, then I believe that you have to have alternatives. You must be able to say there will be a way to give senior citizens the income protection they deserve. And there are alternatives which I believe we should be encouraging:

We can encourage greater savings for retirement by expanding the use of IRA's and Keogh plans.

We need to strengthen our system of private pensions under ERISA.

We can develop innovative financing plans like the reverse annuity mortgage which would help unlock some of the equity senior citizens have in their homes.

We need to vigorously combat the notion that old people can no longer productively contribute to our society.

We can encourage private industry to experiment with programs of retaining older workers on a part-time basis where their skills and experience can still be used.

We can establish experienced worker retraining programs so that the plant worker who is laid off at age 58 does not go on disability or early retirement.

We can find ways of helping displaced homemakers and widows earn extra income so that they do not spend the remainder of their days living in abject proverty.

There are probably countless other ways that we as a society could help our elderly fend for themselves without paying an additional dime in Social Security benefits. But the Administration did not propose these alternatives.

I find that distressing because I think the Administration views our senior citizens as a drain on our society rather than as an asset waiting to be utilized. We assume because they are older, perhaps more frail and not able to work 40 hours a week, that perhaps they are ready to retire and that they have nothing left to offer.

The Administration says that everyone has to sacrifice in order to get this economy moving again. I agree but let us not forget that the people who retire in 1982 were born in 1920 or earlier. They spent their adolescence in the midst of the Great Depression.

The generation which retires next year was also the generation that fought the Second World War. For those of them that came back alive they spent much of the 1940s and 1950s building the prosperity which we, their children, have come to enjoy. This generation knows the meaning of sacrifice because they have had to sacrifice before.

And now after sending their children to college so that they might have a better life, they are looking toward their own retirement and all of a sudden they are being told we can no longer afford them. Social Security has become too expensive. Instead of saying to our parents, "You've given a lot and we are thankful. We are saying we cannot afford the cost of providing for you." I find that ironic, especially when we have a President who epitomizes just how much a senior citizen can offer to our society.

I think that these proposals are a terrible mistake. Senior

citizens in our country today have given a lot. They are entitled to the benefits to which they have contributed for so many years.

I firmly believe that the best measure of the humaneness of a society is the way in which a society treats its elderly. The Social Security Act marks America's commitment to itself. It is the bedrock of a great task ahead of us to preserve and strengthen that foundation. We have a commitment morally as well as financially to maintain that system. But it will take vision and some imagination to do so. Those who would propose slashing benefits to senior citizens seem to view our elderly as a drain on society. That is a mistake.

IV. PLENTY OF REACTION, BUT NO SOLUTION

EDITOR'S INTRODUCTION

On December 16, 1981, both houses of Congress did manage to pass a stop-gap measure that temporarily preserves the financial integrity of Social Security. The act permits the financially troubled Old Age and Survivors Trust Fund (OASI), expected to go broke within the year, to borrow from the more fiscally sound funds (see the Ginzberg article for an explanation of how it works). Due to pressure from the elderly, Congress also restored to present recipients the minimum monthly benefit which had been eliminated in July—the only Congressional reform in response to President Reagan's plan. The President signed this bill and appointed a 15-person bipartisan Social Security Commission, headed by the prominent economist and former Ford/Nixon cabinet member, Alan Greenspan, to make a report on the system. The first article in this section from *Time* describes the very partisan manner in which this bipartisan commission works.

The next two articles in this section deal with reaction to the restoration of the $122 minimum monthly benefit by Congress. The first, a *New York Times* editorial, deplores the restoration of the benefit and analyzes the compromise legislation, warning that difficulties lie ahead and "reality will have to be faced." Next, Mrs. Lou Glasse, Director of the New York State Office of the Aging, rebuts the *New York Times* in a Letter to the Editor, maintaining that it is not "double dippers," but "truly needy" Americans who will lose this money.

Who defeated President Reagan on his Social Security plan and is compounding difficulties in passing a Social Security reform program? Many political analysts credit the "gray lobby"—a demographically growing population of elderly Americans—politically powerful and determined to strengthen, not reduce Social Security benefits. The fourth and fifth articles survey this group of Americans. Starting from the 1920s, Larry Light provides the history of the gray lobby in his *Congressional Quarterly* article. He describes the AARP, the Gray Panthers, and other lobbying organizations for the elderly, who have become a sizable political force to contend with. The next article, from *U.S. News & World Report*, describes the lobbying groups for the elderly and their protest rally on the Capitol steps in Washington on July 21st in response to the Reagan plan.

The gray lobby participated in a White House Conference on the Aging in late November 1981. Its representatives found themselves outvoted on a number of issues and they accused the Administration of packing the conference. The last three articles in this section, from *Time* Magazine, the *Congressional Quarterly,* and the *New York Times,* profile the conference, the delegates, and the controversies. Irwin B. Arieff concentrates his attentions on the champion of the elderly, liberal Representative Claude Pepper (D-Fla.), who has been working tirelessly for the aged for many of his 81 years. Then, William A. Henry III traces the White House Conferences on the Aging through the years and examines the statistics concerning the actual incomes of the elderly, as well as the concept of the "wellderly." And, finally, in revealing the Reagan strategy used at the conference, Warren Weaver Jr. observes in the *New York Times* that "Not everyone can identify readily and sympathetically with women, blacks, veterans, or farmers. But barring untimely demise, everyone inevitably grows old."

A PARTISAN CLASH AT THE BIPARTISAN COMMISSION[1]

The scene: Room 5110 of the Dirksen Senate Office building. The occasion: the first public meeting of the bipartisan National Commission on Social Security Reform to take place since the President and Senate Budget Committee called for $40 billion in cuts in the system over the next three years. The

[1] Article from *Time.* 118:27. My. 24, '82. Copyright 1982 by Time Inc. All rights reserved. Reprinted by permission.

result: a partisan shouting match, with cameras clicking, that symbolized the tensions evoked by this sensitive issue.

Republican Senator John Heinz of Pennsylvania, who is running for a second term this fall, announced that he was tired of hearing that his party was "trying to balance the budget on the backs of Social Security recipients." He proposed separating the program from the overall budget, as one way to avoid "a lot of political posturing." Heinz's proposal drew support from other commissioners, but then the fun began.

Florida Democrat Claude Pepper, 81, who heads the House Select Committee on Aging, wondered if television cameras would be required to leave the meeting after ten minutes. "Absolutely not," said Economist Alan Greenspan, the commission's chairman. The TV crews could stay as long as they liked. Meanwhile, Democratic Senator Daniel Patrick Moynihan of New York was incensed about the entire proceedings. Heinz's proposal was fine for the future, he said, but "we are facing a crisis of the present." Since the Senate Budget Committee "ordered this commission to cut $40 billion, Moynihan complained, "we've been told in advance what we must report." Chimed in Pepper: "People must be in a grave quandary" with talk of $40 billion in cutbacks coming on top of presidential assurances that benefits will be protected. "What are people to believe?" he drawled. "This commission has been compromised." Moynihan was just getting wound up. The Reagan Administration, he fumed, has "terrorized older people into thinking that they won't get their Social Security."

That statement triggered the fury of Colorado's Republican Senator William Armstrong. "I'm dismayed by the conversation that has taken place here," he said. "My colleague from New York on the Senate floor has demagogued this issue from front to back and top to bottom and he is trying to do the same here," he said. "You've tried to emotionalize what should not be an emotional issue. We have done everything to avoid making this a partisan issue," Armstrong declared, just before charging that the proposal for the $40 billion cutback originated with the Democrats.

Pepper demanded that Chairman Greenspan rebuke Armstrong: "If one member can make an assault on another, we become a brawling group." Greenspan mildly reiterated his hope that "we can keep the rhetoric down to an absolute minimum." Wisecracked Republican Senator Robert Dole of Kansas: "We carry on like this all the time on the floor of the House and the Senate."

So went the turbulent first hour of the session, which was only the third meeting of the commission since Reagan proposed its formation last September. The 15 members of the commission—five named by the President and five each by the leadership of the Senate and House—include Robert Ball, former head of the Social Security Administration, AFL-CIO President Lane Kirkland and Robert Beck, chairman of the Prudential Insurance Co.

The commission's ostensible goal is to recommend changes in the Social Security system, but it is not due to report any findings until the end of the year, well after the congressional elections. There is little hope that the commission will reach any kind of consensus, since it has been hampered by the grandstanding of members who are up for re-election, by the intransigence of "gray power" activists like Pepper, who see no real need for reform, and by an untaxing schedule: just one meeting a month. At the commission's first session last February, Chairman Greenspan jocularly suggested that its members might wind up by issuing 15 minority reports. His prediction may yet prove to be true.

SANTA CLAUS? NO, GRANDFATHER CLAUSE[2]

Pensioners on Social Security are breathing easier this week. A House-Senate conference committee broke a deadlock and eliminated any possibility that the Social Security

[2] Reprint of *New York Times* editorial. D. '17, '81. Copyright © 1981, by The New York Times Company. Reprinted by permission.

system would be unable to mail out checks in 1982. But the minor changes that were made in benefits will save only a few hundred million dollars a year. And the bitter struggle for even these modest changes shows how hard it will be to go further.

Last summer President Reagan asked Congress to cut Social Security benefits and tighten eligibility requirements. Fundamental change was needed, he argued, to avoid increasing the payroll tax. Mr. Reagan ran into an instant storm and backed down. But Congress did eliminate, starting in 1982, the $122 minimum monthly benefit for pensioners who did not actually qualify for that amount.

It was a wholly defensible cut. Many of those affected are former part-time workers with good incomes, or retired public employees who worked just long enough in the private sector to qualify for a second pension. Some poor beneficiaries really need the minimum, but they would be eligible for at least as much from the means-tested Supplemental Security Income program. The change would thus have distinguished the truly needy from undeserving middle-income beneficiaries.

That argument, however, does not impress the pensioners' lobbies, which regard any reduction as a betrayal. Nor did it stop House Democrats from using the issue to embarrass the President. The House, switching positions, simply voted to restore the minimum benefit.

That House bill was then sent to conference along with a measure to permit the old-age pension fund to "borrow" from the disability and hospital insurance funds. Inter-fund borrowing was a good idea, the House and Senate conferees agreed; it would give Congress a few more years to find a way to balance the system's accounts. But Senate conferees were determined to end the minimum benefit.

The compromise that was finally struck will eliminate the minimum benefit for future retirees. But a "grandfather" clause allows the three million pensioners already receiving it to keep on getting it. Inter-fund borrowing will be allowed, but only through 1982. That time limit will force Congress to

look again after the 1982 elections, when the risks of demagoguery may abate.

Everyone concerned is putting a good face on the agree-
ment, but the scars show through. The saving is a fraction of
the billions needed to save Social Security from bankruptcy.
A study panel appointed by President Reagan, Senate Majority Leader Baker and House Speaker O'Neill will look for a
better remedy.

The outline of a fair approach has long been clear. Given
the increase in life expectancy, the retirement age for maximum benefits should be slowly increased from 65 to 68. To
eliminate "double-dipping," all government employees
should be required to contribute to Social Security. And, by
some means, benefits should be capped or reduced for retirees
with above-average incomes.

Are these changes politically possible? The haste with
which Congress and the President retreated this year is discouraging. It is hard to believe that another study panel will
agree on an adequate approach when so many others have
failed before. But the clock is ticking. Sometime in the mid-
1980s the money will run out, and one way or another, reality
will have to be faced.

HOW NOT TO FIX THE SOCIAL
SECURITY SYSTEM[3]

The Social Security "minimum benefit" is an important,
and not easily replaced, source of income for some recipients.
As such, it was most disheartening to read your December 17
editorial "Santa Claus? No, Grandfather Clause," which
called the Reagan administration's attempt to remove the
payment "a wholly defensible cut."

The editorial repeats the conclusions that caused Congress to repeal the minimum benefit at the urging of the Rea-

[3] Reprint of Letter to the Editor by Mrs. Lou Glasse, *New York Times*. D. '28, '81.
Copyright © 1981 by The New York Times Company. Reprinted by permission.

gan administration last August. Since then, Congress has discovered the fallacies, but The *Times* uses them still.

There has been a false impression that most of the recipients have been "double-dippers"—persons who receive other benefits, such as government pensions, but are able to qualify for Social Security because they worked for a short time in the private sector.

A Social Security Administration study published by the Congressional Research Service says that only 10 to 12 percent of current minimum-benefit recipients are covered by federal, state or local pensions.

Another fallacy is the claim that none of the "truly needy" will be hurt—your editorial claims they would be "eligible for at least as much from the means-tested Supplemental Security Income program."

The fact is that many needy who would have received the minimum benefit will not be eligible for S.S.I. That program is open only to those over the age of 65, the blind and the disabled. And a single applicant must have no more than $1,500 in assets, house and car allowance excluded.

What about a needy retiree of 62? It should be pointed out that many persons retire because they are forced to, because of ill health or lack of employment opportunities. This situation does not always coincide neatly with a 65th birthday.

A second reason some would not have the minimum benefit replaced by S.S.I. is a great reluctance to apply for a "welfare" program. The minimum benefit is a right provided by the original 1935 Social Security legislation.

The Social Security Administration's Office of Research and Statistics estimated last summer that only about one-quarter of potential S.S.I. recipients would actually apply for and receive benefits if the minimum benefit were eliminated.

Perhaps the most disheartening element of the editorial was its contribution to increasing lack of confidence in the future of the Social Security system.

An Associated Press-NBC poll last spring said that 74 percent of those questioned had little or no confidence that the

Social Security system will have the money to pay them retirement benefits when they quit working, or are forced to leave the work force.

It is that very lack of confidence that has made the efforts to deal with the system's problems a political matter. The public has now been shown that the present Administration and a cowed Congress are capable of cutting off benefits to recipients with only a few months' notice. I applaud the Congress's reconsideration of its action, but that flip-flop also adds to the public's insecurity.

All of this has obscured the most important message: Social Security has real problems, but they can be solved. The problems must not be solved by hastily drawn and politically motivated short-term plans.

Your editorial carries the impression that Social Security is unalterably headed downhill and that little can be done to halt the slide, short of cutting benefits. The fact is that the system's short-term problems can be dealt with through reasoned changes, including interfund borrowing through the coming decade. The more serious problem which may be looming on the horizon several decades from now should be dealt with carefully, and on the basis of facts.

THE ORGANIZED ELDERLY: A POWERFUL LOBBY[4]

Many organizations of the elderly that lobby Congress on legislation try to stay out of partisan politics.

They figure that sympathy for senior citizens and respect for the clout of older Americans on Election Day guarantee them an attentive audience. "It's better to be non-partisan," said Nick Willard, a lobbyist for the American Association of Retired Persons.

[4] Reprint of magazine article by Larry Light, staff writer. *Congressional Quarterly.* 39:2345. N. 28, '81. Copyright 1981, Congressional Quarterly Inc. Reprinted by permission.

"There are no political action committees" (PACs) among old people's groups, he said.

The lack of a campaign-funding apparatus doesn't seem to diminish the lobbying power of the elderly.

"They do wield a certain amount of influence," said Representative Daniel A. Mica (D-Fla.) a member of the House Select Committee on Aging. While not united on all issues, he said, "when they combine, they are very effective."

History of Aging Lobby

The organized elderly became a fixture on the Washington scene only in the 1960s. Before that, others worked to enact government programs for them.

In the 1920s, the Fraternal Order of Eagles lobbied state legislatures to set up pension plans in their states.

California was the center of activity to establish pension protection for the aged. In 1929, following extensive lobbying by the Eagles, the state started the first mandatory system in the nation. Novelist Upton Sinclair, running as a Democrat for governor in 1934, made increasing the meager state benefit ($23 monthly) a cornerstone of his unsuccessful campaign.

The push for a nationwide pension, headed by a California physician named Francis Townsend, began in the early 1930s. The Townsend movement agitated for creation of the Social Security system, which Franklin D. Roosevelt adopted as his own cause.

Oddly enough, organized labor initially opposed pension schemes. In the early 1900s, the American Federation of Labor depicted them as socialistic. But by the Roosevelt era, unions were all for Social Security, and in the 1960s they led the struggle to enact Medicare.

Out of the Medicare fight emerged a "gray lobby" that went on to fight legislative battles over lifting mandatory retirement, expanding Social Security benefits and—most recently—restoring the $122 minimum monthly Social Security benefit for current recipients.

The Key Players

The largest group working for the aged is the 12-million-member American Association of Retired Persons (AARP), whose Washington headquarters has its own ZIP code. It has an affiliate, the National Retired Teachers Association (NRTA), which actually founded the AARP in 1958. Another prominent group, the National Council of Senior Citizens, was created by labor in the 1960s. And then there are the Gray Panthers, who do little lobbying in Washington, preferring to work for the elderly at the local level.

"We all agree on the role of the public sector in maintaining the current Social Security benefits," said Jack Ossofsky, executive director of the National Council on the Aging.

Through the Legislative Council of Aging Organizations, an umbrella group chaired by Ossofsky, 23 of these bodies have been working this year to reauthorize the Older Americans Act (which provides food and jobs), maintain funding for "Section 202" housing construction loans and restore Social Security minimum benefits.

Some differences do exist among the organizations. The AARP, for example, wants to eliminate the requirement that reduces a person's Social Security benefits if he or she holds a job. The National Council of Senior Citizens disagrees, saying that someone still able to work should not be depleting the Social Security fund.

How Much Paternalism?

As a strong electoral force with a potent lobbying presence, the elderly are taken seriously in the world of public affairs. But some wonder whether the aged have not exchanged the bonds of economic uncertainty for those of government paternalism.

Federal aid is "increasingly threatening to older people today," writes Brandeis history Professor David H. Fischer.

"We live ... in a world of bureaucratized aging, where choices and decisions are made not by private individuals, but by public officials."

Indeed, the emphasis that the lobby groups place on government programs has sometimes provoked angry criticism from their politically conservative members.

For example, when the AARP in the 1970s endorsed federally paid health insurance for every American, it received a cascade of protests from its own members.

But with the percentage of those 65 and over expected to grow enormously over the next few decades, chances are that federal aid to the elderly will become even more important to the "gray lobby" in the years to come.

SENIOR CITIZENS PUT ON THE WAR PAINT[5]

Angered and dismayed by Ronald Reagan's proposal to cut Social Security, older Americans are striking back.

Their scheduled protest rally on the Capitol steps July 21 was only the latest jab in what is rapidly becoming a classic legislative battle—a popular President versus one of the nation's most effective lobbying forces.

Advocates for the aged say they will spare no effort to block Reagan or anyone else from reducing Social Security payments for present or future retirees. The President, backed by many experts, is warning that benefits must be scaled back to avoid bankrupting the system.

Congress is under heavy pressure to do something this year to rescue the financially troubled program, which has been paying out more in benefits than it collects in taxes. An infusion from the Treasury and another boost in taxes virtually have been ruled out as economically and politically in-

[5] Reprint of staff-written magazine article, *U.S. News & World Report.* 91:33–4. Jl. 27, '81. Copyright 1981, U.S. News & World Report, Inc.

feasible remedies. With Reagan supporting it as the least objectionable choice, a reduction in benefits could be hard to stop.

Still, few are underestimating the lobby that has so successfully fought similar legislation in the past.

When the Carter administration proposed relatively minor cuts in Social Security two years ago, the elderly reacted so strongly that no one in Congress would even introduce the bill.

The Reagan plan, announced May 12, has triggered an even more vehement response from older citizens. Working individually and through scores of organized groups, they have swamped congressional offices with tons of mail, thousands of telephone calls and hundreds of personal visits.

Swift Response

Relying almost entirely on grass-roots persuasion, the elderly and their supporters began mobilizing within hours after the Reagan plan was announced. The combined National Retired Teachers Association and American Association of Retired Persons fired off "legislative alerts" to 14,000 volunteer leaders, urging them to contact lawmakers and to recruit other association members, friends and relatives to do the same.

The National Council of Senior Citizens mailed 10,000 large-type "Seniorgrams" to officials in its network of 4,000 clubs. Save Our Security, a coalition of some 90 unions, religious groups and others, used mail, telephones and personal meetings to alert the 35 million people it purports to represent.

Also swinging into action were the Gray Panthers, a small but colorful activist group headed by Maggie Kuhn, a grandmotherly 75-year-old. A popular speaker, Kuhn tells her contemporaries: "We have nothing to lose. We can take risks. We can just raise hell. No one can stop us."

The outpouring of anguish and anger was so great that, eight days after Reagan's announcement, the Republican-controlled Senate unanimously declared its opposition to any plan that "precipitously and unfairly" reduces benefits. House Democrats, seizing on the potentially explosive political issue, accused the Administration of an "unconscionable breach of faith."

What makes the elderly one of the most respected and feared special interests on Capitol Hill?

Its sheer size—more than 47 million Americans are in the over-55 age group—assures the lobby of a full hearing from Congress. Older citizens also are known for making the fullest use of their power. As Senator William Proxmire (D-Wis.) puts it: "They have a very big constituency, they're active— and they vote."

Last year, senior Americans, representing 29 percent of the voting-age population, cast more than 33 percent of the ballots for President.

Such statistics give added impact to the small army of lobbyists that roams the corridors of Congress in behalf of the nation's elderly. "We make mention of our size and the fact that it's the group of people from which you get the largest percentage of the vote," says William Driver, executive vice chairman of Save Our Security, which opposes any cuts in retirement benefits. "We also impress upon congressmen that we're urging our members to oppose anyone who favors the cuts."

Lawmakers contend they are swayed not by threats of political retribution, direct or indirect, but by the heart-rending appeals that flood in from individuals whose fixed incomes are being devoured by inflation or who feel the government's promise of old-age security is being broken.

Representative Lynn Martin (R-Ill.) explains: "If someone calls and says, 'Vote this way or else,' most of us would say, 'You just watch us,' But if someone calls and says, 'Am I going to be able to pay the rent next month?' that's really powerful."

What Cuts Will Mean

Sacks full of mail pour in weekly to congressional offices, particularly that of Representative Claude Pepper (D-Fla.), chairman of the House Select Committee on Aging, an octogenarian and a vigorous advocate of older people's rights.

Typical of the mail is this letter from a Lombard, Illinois, resident to Representative John Erlenborn (R-Ill.): "I've worked for 40 years in a dirty, noisy factory. My wife and I have skimped and done without to raise and school our children. All of my working life I've had Social Security taxes taken from my pay. And now with my health going and almost ready to retire at age 62 and maybe breathe fresh air and not have noise pounding all the time, I'm being told that my Social Security will be cut. It's not fair."

While many letters are spontaneous, others are orchestrated in Washington by lobbying organizations for the elderly. "We find that the best way to get to a congressman is through his constituents," says William R. Hutton, executive director of the National Council of Senior Citizens.

Representative Richard Gephardt (D-Mo.) adds that it's the "frequency and intensity" of such contact that really makes the difference.

Grass-roots pressure and letter writing are not the only tools employed by the elderly lobby. One common tactic is the public demonstration. Besides the July 21 rally at the Capitol, the Gray Panthers have been holding demonstrations around the country and staging vigils across the street from the White House.

Lobbyists for senior-citizens groups and experts such as SOS's Driver and Robert M. Ball, both former Social Security commissioners, are testifying at congressional hearings and plying lawmakers with reams of reports and statistics.

Still, despite all its vaunted power, the senior-citizen lobby may prove inadequate in preventing at least a minimal loss of retirement benefits. Even some of the groups representing the elderly are beginning to have doubts about a strategy of total opposition.

Although officially the lobby continues to maintain a steadfast opposition to any cuts, there are rumblings from within about the ultimate futility of taking, as one lobbyist described it, "a head-in-the-sand approach" to the system's financing problems. Declares Peter W. Hughes, of the NRTA/AARP: "We're not saying, 'No cuts.' But we'd like to help direct where they will be made, make sure that they are prospective and try to keep them as minimal as possible."

CLAUDE PEPPER: CHAMPION OF THE AGING[6]

Austerity may be all the rage in Congress today, but Representative Claude Pepper (D.-Fla.) is an unabashed advocate of big spending.

Throughout a political career that has spanned more than half a century, Pepper—whatever the fashion of the time—has remained dedicated to the proposition that the federal government should play a central role in improving the health and welfare of its citizens. . . .

As chairman of the House Select Committee on Aging and honorary co-chairman of the White House conference, he has spent much of the past year criticizing President Reagan for his treatment of senior citizens. First he attacked Reagan's cuts in federal programs for the aged. Then he charged the Administration was plotting to manipulate the conference to Reagan's political advantage.

Pepper maintains that instead of cutting programs for the aging, Reagan should be pouring additional billions into new programs aimed at improving the health, housing, nutrition and mobility of older Americans.

He contends that conference delegates, if left to their own devices, probably would recommend such an agenda. But the

[6] Reprint of magazine article by Irwin B. Arieff, staff writer. *Congressional Quarterly.* 39:2342. N. 28, '81. Copyright 1981, Congressional Quarterly Inc. Reprinted by permission.

White House is trying to turn the conference into a cheering section for the President's views, Pepper charges.

"They want a whitewashing, basically," he said in a recent interview.

Pepper has slowed his pace over the years. His face is deeply lined, he is quite hard of hearing and his heart beats with the aid of an artificial valve.

Still, he relishes a lively political scrap.

"I am enjoying it," Pepper says of his activist role on behalf of the aging. "I'm 81, and the Lord's been good to me. And if I can repay my fellow Americans for the kindness the Lord has shown me, then I'll be glad to do it."

Pepper's role as advocate for the aging has brought him political benefits. He has been showered with favorable publicity and hailed by groups representing the elderly, many of whom have recently begun referring to him as "Mr. Aging."

Pepper feels his efforts eventually may pay off for other Democrats, as well, Older Americans, he maintains, constitute a potentially enormous voting bloc. Most have tended to vote Republican in the past but are ripe for a switch, he says, promising that the Democrats will have a "firm program" to attract their votes in 1982.

High Cost of Crusading

Being a liberal has not been without its hazards. Twice in the past, Pepper's crusading has cost him a political post.

The son of a sharecropper, Pepper worked his way through the University of Alabama and Harvard Law School and in 1929 won a seat in the Florida Legislature. But his stay there was brief. He was defeated after a single two-year term after opposing a resolution condemning Mrs. Herbert Hoover because she had invited a black man to the White House for tea.

In 1950, he repeated the experience on a grander scale, losing a seat in the U.S. Senate to fellow Democrat and former protégé George A. Smathers (House, 1947–51; Senate, 1951–69).

Pepper was first elected to a two-year term in the Senate in 1936 and won re-election in 1938 and 1944. But he lost the 1950 Democratic primary in a race that has come to be known as one of the dirtiest in American history.

In the Senate, Pepper had been a fervent ally of President Roosevelt and his New Deal, and had later criticized President Truman for surrounding himself with "reactionary advisers." An early advocate of war with Nazi Germany, he met with Joseph Stalin in Moscow in 1945 and became convinced the Russians were disarming and wanted peace.

As a result of his controversial views, Pepper was tarred in 1950 as "Red Pepper," "soft on communism" and a "nigger lover." Even his looks became an issue when Smathers' supporters passed out horn-rimmed glasses with false noses. He joked at the time: "They can call me a red and a black, but when they attack my beauty, that's too much."

Following his defeat, he built up a law practice in Florida, but he never lost the desire to return to Washington. His opportunity came in 1962, when he won election to the House from a newly formed district in the Miami area that had one of the highest median ages in the country. He has won re-election to every subsequent Congress.

Pepper is the No. 2 Democrat on the House Rules Committee, in line to become chairman in January 1983, when Richard Bolling (D-Mo.) retires.

Will Pepper still be around then? He jokes that he is contemplating retirement in the year 2000, when he will be 100 years old.

HOW POORLY OFF ARE THE ELDERLY?[7]

The first two White House Conferences on Aging were gatherings of generally like-minded advocates, assembled at

---

[7] Reprint of magazine article by William A. Henry III. *Time Magazine.* 118:37. D. 14, '81.

federal expense to lobby the federal government for more money for the elderly. In 1961 the conference helped build momentum for the passage of Medicare and Medicaid. The 1971 session spurred Congress to a sharp increase in Social Security benefits. But this year, with the White House committed to reducing spending on social services, the delegates were far from like-minded. At times they were as fiery and unruly as college protesters in the '60s.

The conference started with shrill accusations that the Administration had "rigged" committee assignments to affirm President Reagan's views. Worried about the growing backlash against the White House, President Reagan made an unscheduled appearance to dispel doubts that he was "somehow an enemy of my own generation." The conclave ended Thursday with shouts of protest as 2,266 delegates were compelled to approve or reject a package of 600 often contradictory resolutions with a single yes or no vote.

On the biggest issue, Social Security, there was a succession of committee votes alternately favoring and opposing the use of general tax revenues to fund the system; both those conflicting positions were endorsed in the final mass vote on the 14 committee reports.

Amid the chaos both sides claimed victory. President Reagan declared he was "pleased." Yet such advocates of the elderly as Cyril Brickfield, 62, executive director of the American Association of Retired Persons, and Maggie Kuhn, 76, founder of the Gray Panthers, called the 60-page conference report "a liberal document." In fact, the conference did endorse, albeit loosely, nearly all of the "eight for the '80s" goals proposed by a consortium of 25 elderly groups. Among the aims: more access to full-time and part-time work; home delivery of services rather than use of nursing facilities; an eventual but undefined "national health care plan." On two pivotal issues, however, the conference adopted positions urged by Reagan: it did not entirely rule out benefit cuts for future recipients of Social Security, and it did not endorse immediate passage of national health insurance.

Perhaps the most significant debate took place apart from

the conference, among statisticians and researchers. The Reagan administration has reopened a question that elderly advocates had considered long settled: Just how needy are older Americans? In contrast to what the White House claims is a stereotypic view that the elderly are destitute, enfeebled, neglected and unfed, the Reaganauts have been promoting the image of the "wellderly." Most older Americans, the Reagan team says, live in houses they own, on adequate incomes, in good health and with sufficient companionship. That image appeals to the pride of the elderly and their desire for self-reliance; it also undercuts support for major new benefits.

The concept of the "wellderly" found an unlikely and perhaps uneasy ally on the eve of the conference: the National Council on the Aging, an elderly advocacy group, which commissioned a poll on elderly well-being from Louis Harris. His company sampled 3,437 adults, including 540 over the age of 65. Harris' conclusion: "On every single issue tested, the elderly are perceived as being in much more desperate shape than they actually are." Some 48 percent say they have more income than they need; 66 percent own their homes, and most have paid off the mortgage. Although fully 63 percent rely on Social Security as their biggest source of income, 88 percent have some savings, and they report less need than younger people to dip into savings to pay bills.

These statistics may reflect lower expectations among the elderly. In Harris' sample the median household income for all Americans was $20,000, while for the elderly it was only $8,600. Further, the Harris poll found that while elderly men had a median household income of $11,000, the median for women was $6,700, for blacks $5,000 and for Hispanics $5,600. Harris' poll especially pointed up the problems of women, who represent a disproportionate 78 percent of the unfortunate group with incomes below $5,000 a year.

The conference's most rousing episode was a march down a corridor of the Sheraton Washington Hotel led by Democratic Congressman Claude Pepper, 81, of Florida to the doors of the Economics Committee, which was considering recommendations for revising the Social Security system.

While Pepper stepped aside to negotiate a compromise, hundreds of supporters stayed to chant and sing *We Shall Overcome*. The compromise was as inconclusive as much of the rest of the conference: it opposed any reduction in current Social Security benefits, but failed to define whether a change in the complicated formulas would constitute a reduction; it opposed cutbacks for future recipients, but may have poked a loophole in the social safety net by asking only that Congress and the President "make every possible and fiscally reasonable effort" to maintain today's level of benefits.

The Social Security compromise indicated that the Administration may have underestimated the common-sense conservatism of the elderly, who gave 60 percent of their votes to Reagan. Efforts to manipulate the conference, some delegates insisted, ended up hurting the Administration's cause. Said Milton Tupper, 67, a retired Los Angeles businessman: "They could have played a tape from Reagan in which he said, 'I hear there have been some complaints. I have asked the secretary to let you vote on each resolution.' He would have had a chorus of yeses." But the elderly should be flattered by the White House's meddling. If nothing else, it proved that they are a political force to be reckoned with—and even feared.

CONCERNS OF OLDER AMERICANS ADD UP TO BIG-STAKE POLITICS[8]

For a quarter of a century and longer, the elderly have been trying to gain recognition as an entity in American life. They have formed organizations, hired lobbyists, boasted about their numbers and influence, elected friends and defeated enemies, sought and won special treatment from the government.

[8] Reprint of newspaper article by Warren Weaver Jr., staff reporter. *New York Times* D. 6, '81. Copyright © 1981 by The New York Times Company. Reprinted by permission.

As was the case for other special interest groups, their progress has been incremental, with few dramatic break-throughs. Other groups with problems perceived as more pressing have launched more strident appeals. Not surprisingly, then, recognition that the elderly are the fastest-growing segment of the population and among the most politically active has been slow in coming.

But history may well record that 1981 was a watershed year for the elderly and their political apparatus. In September, the self-styled "aging network" dealt President Reagan his only major legislative defeat, forcing him to withdraw from Congressional consideration his proposals to reduce Social Security benefits. Then last week, delegates to the White House Conference on Aging forced the Reagan administration to acknowledge that the concerns of elderly Americans had moved center-stage. The Republicans had tried to assume operating control of the conference. Their success was only partial, and the considerable effort involved to achieve it was a tribute to the importance contemporary politicians attach to their older constituents.

Previous conferences on aging—in 1961 just before Dwight D. Eisenhower left office and in 1971 during Richard M. Nixon's first term—were relatively placid affairs. Proponents of improved pension or health care benefits vied for attention, but the incumbent Republican administrations remained above the fray. Not so in 1981. To the astonishment of some delegates and the anger of others, the Reagan administration decided to try making its mark on the conference, to the extent possible. Administration officials apparently thus hoped to minimize delegate criticism of the President for his Social Security proposals and budget cuts.

The Reagan Gambit

That such criticisms would come was highly likely. Some 1,800 conference delegates were in place before President Reagan took office. Appointed by governors and members of the last Congress, they were likely to produce a Democratic majority overall. Moreover, advocates for the elderly tend to support more federal spending; as a result, Republicans among them are frequently not of the conservative Reagan persuasion.

A reading of the conference record and confidential documents that emerged during the week makes clear the Administration's tactics and strategy. The Republican National Committee commissioned a telephone survey of conference delegates to test political loyalty. When word of the project leaked out the telephoning ended, but the probe for Reagan loyalists continued by mail. According to a letter from the Texas governor's office, the Republicans were looking for delegates "who would put loyalty to the President ahead of their commitment to the elderly and who would not take offense at the involvement of the Republican Party."

The Secretary of Health and Human Services, Richard S. Schweiker, under whose jurisdiction the conference fell, eventually added about 400 delegates, almost all of whom were Republicans. Political operatives assigned the bulk of these Reagan reliables to 3 of the 14 conference committees, thus creating safe majorities on the panels dealing with the significant issues: Social Security, health care and the impact of the economy on the elderly.

Rules were promulgated that made it impossible for the conference to alter committee decisions, short of voting down all committee reports at the closing session. In each of the target panels, "favorable" delegates were made coordinators, whips and deputies, and a plan of attack was devised. It was no accident, then, that the first delegate recognized in the Social Security Committee was Bruce Nestande of California, who was later revealed to be the Reagan whip for that panel.

Mr. Nestande proposed a resolution condemning the use of general fund revenues to bolster the impoverished retirement system, a major point of Reagan doctrine. After spirited debate, the proposal was approved, 111 to 34. Delegates such as Jacob Clayman of the National Council of Senior Citizens and Bert Seidman of the A.F.L.-C.I.O. were stunned. Confident that a majority of all delegates actually opposed the measure, they were helpless to reverse the committee vote in the conference's closing plenary session. So it went in the other two Reagan-majority committees. Resolutions designed to hold down spending for Medicare and Medicaid and to express support for fighting inflation through a balanced budget were easily approved, automatically becoming part of the final conference report.

The Delegate Defense

But delegates representing the major organizations of elderly citizens, recognizing the Administration's strategy early on, counterattacked. They rewrote resolutions that would lose in the pro-Reagan committees so the proposals could be considered by panels where the political balance was more equitable. The Committee on Older Women, with its almost unlimited jurisdiction, became particularly active in this regard.

Thus, when President Reagan surprised the conference with a visit Tuesday, key committees seemed to be giving him a victory. But by the end of business Thursday, the combined report of all panels was weighted with recommendations contrary to White House policy: no Social Security benefit cuts, more Medicare and Medicaid spending, restoration of federal budget cuts on programs affecting the elderly.

The conference's struggle over Social Security mirrored the battle taking place in Congress this year. At the President's urging, the Republican Senate majority, insisting there is a financial crisis in the retirement system, called for major corrective actions to be taken now. The Democratic House had denied any crisis and proposed only minor tinkering. The House position claimed the louder voice in the conference's final report.

Speaking to the delegates, President Reagan said he would soon name his appointees to a 15-member task force on Social Security designed to resolve the Congressional deadlock. Senate and House leaders of both parties will also be appointing task force members. The group, President Reagan has said, will be bipartisan. Delegates who accused him of trying to "stack the deck" last week will certainly watch to make sure. And they may not be alone.

If elderly people have gained national recognition as a significant political constituency, it is almost certainly due in part to a unique advantage they enjoy over other special interest groups. Not everyone can identify readily and sympathetically with women, blacks, veterans or farmers. But barring untimely demise, everyone inevitably grows old.

BIBLIOGRAPHY

An asterisk (*) preceding a reference indicates that the article or part of it has been reprinted in this book.

Books, Pamphlets and Documents

Ball, Robert M. Social Security today and tomorrow. Columbia University Press. '78.

Bush, George F. et al. The crisis in Social Security: problems and prospects. Institute for Contemporary Study. '78.

Campbell, Colin D., ed. Financing Social Security. American Enterprise Institute. '79.

Campbell, Rita Ricardo. Social Security: Promise and reality. Hoover Institution Press. '77.

Cohen, Wilbur J. and Friedman, Milton. Social Security: universal or selective. The American Enterprise Institute. '72.

Colberg, Marshall R. Social Security retirement test: right or wrong? American Enterprise Institute. '78.

Derthick, Martha. Policymaking for Social Security. The Brookings Institution. '80.

Dickinson, Peter A. Get more money from Social Security. Grosset and Dunlap. '82.

Drucker, Peter F. The unseen revolution: how pension fund socialization came to America. Harper & Row. '76.

Editorial Research Reports. Vol. 1, No. 24. Je. 29, '79. Social Security reassessment. Richard C. Schroeder.

Editorial Research Reports. Vol. 1. No. 9. Mr. 6, '81. Retirement income in jeopardy. Richard C. Schroeder.

Editorial Research Reports. Vol. 11, No. 12:728+. S. 25, '81. Women and aging; inequities in Social Security. Jean Rosenblatt.

Ferrara, Peter J. Reforming Social Security. (Cato Public Policy Research Monograph No. 4.) Cato Institute. '82.

Graebner, William. A history of retirement: the meaning and function of an American institution. Yale University Press. '80.

Jorgensen, James. The graying of America: retirement and why you can't afford it. The Dial Press. '81.

Jorgensen, James. Your retirement income. Scribner. '82.

Kaplan, Robert S. Indexing Social Security: an analysis of the issues. American Enterprise Institute. '78.

Levy, Mickey D. Tax treatment of Social Security. American Enterprise Institute. '80.

Meyer, Charles W. Social Security disability insurance problems of unexpected growth. American Enterprise Institute. '79.

Munnell, Alicia H. The future of Social Security. The Brookings Institution. '77.

Myers, Robert. Social Security. Richard D. Irwin, Inc. '81.

New York State Task Force on Social Security. Keeping Social Security strong—analysis and recommendations. '81.

President's Commission On Pension Policy. Coming of age: toward a national retirement income policy. F. 26, '81. US Government.

Robertson, A. Haeworth. The coming revolution in Social Security. Security Press. '81.

*Schlesinger, Arthur M. The coming of the New Deal. Houghton Mifflin. '58.

Skidmore, Felicity, ed. Social Security financing. MIT Press. '81.

Social Security benefits including Medicare, January 1, 1982. Commerce Clearing House. '81.

Stein, Bruno. Social Security and pensions in transition: understanding the American retirement system. Free Press. '80.

Von Furstenberg, George M., ed. Capital investment and saving. Vol. I: Social Security versus private saving. Ballinger Publishers. '79.

Webster, Bryce and Perry, Robert L. The complete Social Security handbook: the clearest, most detailed guide to learning how and when to get all the benefits due you. Everest House. '82.

Williams, C. Arthur. Economic and Social Security: social insurance and other approaches. Ronald Press. '81.

Wynne, Edward. Social Security: a reciprocity system under pressure. (Westview Special Studies in Contemporary Social Issues.) Westview Press. '80.

PERIODICALS

America. 145:391. D. 19, '81. Senior power.

Business Week. p 52. My. 25, '81. Can Reagan revolutionize Social Security? V. Cahan and S. H. Wildstrom.

Business Week. p 121. Je. 1, '81. A stumble over Social Security. Lee Walczak.

Business Week. p 116. S. 28, '81. Battle over repairing Social Security.

Business Week. p 108. N. 30, '81. How to straighten out any Social Security snafus. Donald H. Dunn.

Business Week. p 50–1. My. 24, '82. Why Social Security is still a budget hangup.

Business Week. p 72+. My. 31, '82. Saying no to Social Security (pullout by non-profit groups).

Changing Times. 34:64–8. Je. '80. Denied your Social Security benefits: Appeal!

Christian Century. 98:1151–2. N. 11, '81. Conference on aging: realistic expectations. A. L. Meiburg.

°Congressional Digest. 60:195–222. Ag./S. '81. Controversy over financing Social Security and Pro & Con: Should congress act now to curtail the future growth of Social Security benefits?

°Congressional Quarterly Weekly Report. 39:2321–84. N. 28, '81. The aging of America.

Consumers report. 46:503–10. S. '81. Your stake in the fight over Social Security.

Economist. 275:28+. Je. 7, '80. Just a mirage?

Fifty Plus. 20:44+. O. '80. Social Security: unfair to women. P. J. Ognibene.

Fifty Plus. 21:18–19. Jl. '81. Will there be a war between old and young? P. J. Ognibene.

Fifty Plus. 21:20. Jl. '81. Honeymoon is over but Reagon may try to cut Social Security again. Jack Anderson.

Fifty Plus. 21:12. S. '81. Social Security cuts: why is Reagan accentuating the negative. Jack Anderson.

Fifty Plus. 21:34–5. S. '81. Can Social Security be saved? P. J. Ognibene.

Fifty Plus. 21:10. O. '81. Who says minimum benefit doesn't pay. Jack Anderson.

Fifty Plus. 22:12. F. '82. Spice of life: Social Security's data tapes need better housekeeping. Jack Anderson.

Fifty Plus. 22:16–17. F. '82. Raising hell (Investigation of fraud by Inspector General's office of the Dept. of Health and Human Services). Jack Anderson.

Fifty Plus. 22:44–5. F. '82. Did it do more harm than good? B. B. Greene.

Fifty Plus. 22:10. Mr. '82. How the Republicans whipped the Conference on Aging into shape. Jack Anderson.

°Forbes. 125:39–40. My. 26, '80. The shocking shape of things to come. Ashby Bladen.

Forbes. 126:61–2. D. 8, '80. Social Security: don't count on it.

Fortune. 102:97+. Ag. 11, '80. Onward and upward. D. Seligman.

°Fortune. 102:34–9. Ag. 25, '80. How to save Social Security. A. F. Ehrbar.

Glamour. 78:130+. Mr. '80. Biggest women's issue this year. M. B. Peter.

Human Ecology Forum. 12:14–19. Summer '81. Social Security: how secure is it? Z. P. Henderson.

Journal of Economic Issues. 15:477–87. Je. '81. Earlier retirement and the older worker. Harold Wolozin.

McCalls. 108:42. Je. '81. How Social Security shortchanges women. Miriam Schneir.

McCalls. 109:76. Mr. '82. Social Security errors could cost you money. Richard Blodgett.

Ms. 10:81–4. Jl. '81. Everything you have to know about Social Security. Miriam Schneir.

Nation. 234:111–13. Social Security goes private. W. K. Tabb.

National Retired Teachers Association/American Association of Retired Persons. The future of Social Security; what Americans think. Poll released in November, 1981.

National Review. 33:597–8. My. 29, '81. Rescuing Social Security.

National Review. 33:860–1. Jl. 24, '81. Peterson on entitlements. William F. Buckley Jr.

National Review. 34:605. My. 28, '82. The 1983 budget and Social Security.

New Leader. 64:5–7. Je. 1, '81. Threat to Social Security. W. J. Cohen.

New Republic. 185:4. Ag. 1–8, '81. TRB from Washington.

New Republic. 185:15–16. Ag. 1–8, '81. Pension tensions. S. Chapman.

*Newsweek. 98:40. S. 21, '81. Cuts in Social Security.

Newsweek. 98:71. O. 26, '81. Saving Social Security. L. C. Thurow.

Newsweek. 99:61. Mr. 15, '82. Social Security: old computers.

Newsweek. 99:24–6. My. 24, '82. The third rail of politics. T. Morganthau.

Newsweek. 99:26. My. 24, '82. Redesigning Social Security. L. C. Thurow.

*New York Times. D. 6, '81. Concerns of older Americans add up to big stakes politics. Warren Weaver Jr.

*New York Times. Editorial. D. 17, '81. Santa Claus? No, grandfather clause.

*New York Times. D. '28, '81. Letter to the editor: How not to fix the Social Security system. Lou Glasse.

New York Times. p 11. Ja. 9, '82. Medicare recipients may have to pay 10 percent of hospital costs.

New York Times. p A13. Ja. 13, '82. Echoes of the Conference on Aging still heard in capital.

New York Times. p A12. Ja. 15, '82. Talk of revamping the Social Security system.

New York Times. p 21. Ja. 17, '82. European and U.S. Social Security compared.

New York Times. 1:1–2. F. 28, '82. Social Security cost-of-living benefits may be trimmed.

New York Times. p A15:1–3. Ap. 2, '82. A warning on Social Security check delays.

New York Times. p A18. Ap. 16, '82. Senator Baker now dubious on limiting Social Security rise.

New York Times. 1:4. Ap. 24, '82. Bolstering the Social Security system with taxes.

New York Times. B4:5–6. My. 7, '82. Medicaid fraud indictments.

New York Times. 9:1–4. My. 8, '82. The Social Security issue.

New York Times. 1:1–2. My. 9, '82. A cutoff in disability benefits under Social Security program.

New York Times. Editorial. p A30. My. 12, '82. Your pension or your vote.

New York Times. p A18. My. 14, '82. Pros and cons of removing Social Security from the budget.

New York Times. p 46. My. 15, '82. Social Security issue divides Republicans in Congress.

New York Times. p B6. My. 19, '82. Q. & A.: Rep. J. J. Pickle on Social Security's troubles.

New York Times. Letter to the Editor. p 22. Je. 5, '82. Don't tamper with Social Security benefits. Nat Berkowitz.

New York Times. p 25+. Je. 5, '82. Queens elderly gather to hear their defender. Leslie Bennetts.

New York Times Magazine. p 125–31. N. 29, '81. Courtly champion of America's elderly. John Egerton.

New York Times Magazine. p 40+. Ja. 17, '82. No more free lunch for the middle class. Peter Peterson.

Public Interest. 58:102–19. Winter '80. Why Social Security is in trouble. Nathan Keyfitz.

Quarterly Journal of Economics. 96:505–29. Ag. '81. Social Security and the retirement decision. V. P. Crawford and D. M. Lilien.

*Saturday Evening Post. 254:38+. Ja./F. '82. The cashing of Social Security checks for dead relatives. Nick Thimmesch.

*Scientific America. 246:51–4. Ja. '82. The Social Security system. Eli Ginzberg.

Social Service Review. 53:655–71. D. '79. White House conferences on the aged. D. Vinyard.

Social Service Review. 54:92–107. Mr. '80. Analysis of HEW's proposals on Social Security. M. N. Ozawa.

Socioeconomic Newsletter. VII, 4:1. Je./Jl. '82. Social Security: Young vs. old.

*Time. 117:24–5. My. 25, '81. A slash at Social Security.

Time. 117:28. My. 25, '81. Right time for boldness. Hugh Sidey.

Time. 118:50. Ag. 10, '81. Proposing a 2% solution.

*Time. 119:16–20+. My. 24, '82. A debt-threatened dream. G. J. Church.

*Time. 119:27. My. 24, '82. A partisan clash at the bipartisan commission.

USA Today. 110:15–16. S. '81. Supply side approach to Social Security. B. R. Schiller.

*U.S. News & World Report. 90:26–8. My. 25, '81. Changes to expect in your Social Security.

U.S. News & World Report. 90:92. Je. 8, '81. Social Security flare up. Marvin Stone.

U.S. News & World Report. 91:41–2. Jl. 20, '81. The battle to save Social Security.

*U.S. News & World Report. 91:33–4. Jl. 27, '81. Senior citizens put on the war paint.

*U.S. News & World Report. 91:35. Jl. 27, '81. "Pro and con: raise the retirement age; interview with Rita Ricardo-Campbell and Betty Duskin.

U.S. News & World Report. 91:95–6. D. 28, '81. What's in the wind for Social Security reform? J. M. Hildreth.

*U.S. News & World Report. 92:67–8. F. 1, '82. Those fouled-up Social Security checks (problems with Social Security computer systems). J. M. Hildreth.

U.S. News & World Report. 92:35–6. F. 15, '82. Will Social Security go broke soon? (Interview with J. A. Svahn).

U.S. News & World Report. 92:84. Mr. 15, '82. Social Security takes aim at its creaky computers.

U.S. News & World Report. 92:90. Ap. 26, '82. The great COLA war—what's at stake. J. M. Hildreth.

U.S. News & World Report. 92:81–2. My. 10, '82. Pro and con: limit increases in Social Security? [Domenici (R) vs. Metzenbaum (D)]

14-185